Mystic Tales from the Zohar

Mystic Tales
from the Zohar

Translated with Notes
and Commentary by

Aryeh Wineman

Papercut Art by Diane Palley

The Jewish Publication Society
Philadelphia and Jerusalem

Manufactured in the United States of America

Library of Congress Cataloging-in-Publication Data

Zohar. English. Selections.
  Mystic tales from the Zohar / [translated and edited by] Aryeh
Wineman; papercut art by Diane Palley.
    p. cm.
  Includes bibliographical references.
  ISBN 0–8276–0515–3
  1. Legends, Jewish.   2. Legends, Jewish—History and criticism.
3. Cabala.   4. Mysticism—Judaism.   I. Wineman, Aryeh.   II. Title.
BM530.Z642513   1996
296. 1'6—dc20   95–22295

Designed by Anne O'Donnell
Typeset in ITC Galliard by Bill Frambes Typesetting

10 9 8 7 6 5 4 3 2 1

To Ayala

Publication of this book was made possible through a generous gift from the Morris Perelman Foundation.

Contents

Acknowledgments

As this work approaches completion, I wish to express my gratitude to the National Endowment for the Humanities for a research stipend during the summer of 1989 to further research on the zoharic narratives. That stipend enabled me to pursue work on this subject at the National Library, located at the Hebrew University in Jerusalem, and at the Gershom Scholem Center, situated at the National Library. In addition, I wish to express appreciation to the Harvard University Center for Jewish Studies for a research fellowship during the summer of 1992 that enabled me to complete my work on this project using the resources of the Widener Library at Harvard. I am also thankful to the Library at the State University of New York, Albany, for library privileges as a visiting scholar while working on this project.

A few explanatory words concerning the manuscript: All translations of passages from the Zohar are my own, which I have made from the printed versions of the Zohar. Unless otherwise indicated, references to talmudic sources are from the Babylonian Talmud. And translations of biblical verses in the texts are taken from The Jewish Publication Society translation TANAKH (Philadelphia, 1985), unless the textual context specifically called for an alternative translation.

My appreciation to Dr. Ellen Frankel, Editor-in-Chief of The Jewish Publication Society, for her interest and encouragement in this work and also to Diane Zuckerman, Managing Editor, and Leslie Cohen and Jody Gould, Project Editors, for their efforts in bringing this manuscript to print.

Aryeh Wineman

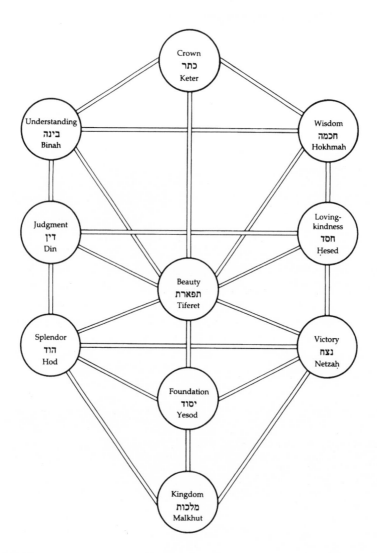

The Sefirotic Tree

Introduction: On the Zoharic Story

The Zohar (the word itself means "brilliant light") is a Jewish medieval mystic text that appeared in late thirteenth-century Christian Spain. Written in an artificial Aramaic, masking a medieval Hebrew, it is a collection of mystical writings including a homiletical commentary on the Torah. The author wrote the Zohar as a pseudepigraphical work, claiming it to be the composition or statement of the teachings and revelations given to Rabbi Simeon bar Yohai, a second-century talmudic sage. For this reason, the Zohar is written in Aramaic, the language of the greater part of the Talmud. Largely as a result of Gershom Scholem's monumental research on the subject, contemporary critical scholars virtually unanimously believe the major part of the Zohar to be the work of Moses ben Shem Tov of Leon.[1]

The Zohar came to acquire virtual canonical status within the world of Kabbalah which, during the sixteenth through eighteenth centuries, came to comprise almost all of world Jewry. In the nineteenth century, the Zohar was severely denigrated by rationalist Western Judaism; the leading Jewish historian of the time, Heinrich Graetz, called it a "book of falsehoods."[2] Because of a growing appreciation of Jewish mysticism today the Zohar is more readily seen as a remarkable text of pronounced poetic qualities and as a vast symbolic complex conveying a distinct and even profound mode of spirituality.

At the core of the Zohar is a theosophical view of being. It focuses upon the dynamic inner life of the divine and upon the drama accompanying the emanation of aspects of the Divine Being and personality *(Sefirot)*—all contained within the infinite Godhead, far beyond the grasp of human thought. The zoharic drama leaves room

1

for the demonic alongside the holy and depicts the higher realms of being—reflected in everything we experience in the world known to us—through images of an interrelationship of aspects of the divine that underlie our world. The zoharic cosmic picture abounds with images of separation and danger, of exile and longing, of love, ecstasy, union, and oneness.

The remarkable literary richness of the Zohar likely accounts in part for the singularly exulted place the book attained within the world of Kabbalah. The zoharic writer grasped the world and the worlds through the lens of an extravagantly colorful, even exotic imagination. The Zohar's theosophical teaching approaches the ultimate issues of existence not in terms of abstract concepts but rather in a manner akin to narrative; its discourse comprises a vast story centered around the pulsating inner life of the Divine Being, the ultimate reality. At times its lengthy homiletic passages are highly descriptive and possess a pronounced lyrical tone. These qualities make the Zohar a kind of expansive prose poem, the fruit of an almost unbounded imagination that draws from layer upon layer of earlier Jewish lore, adding to them the Zohar's own mythic nuances and themes. Probably no other text in the annals of Jewish writing and thought so abounds in archetypal motifs and mythic images and themes, and the Zohar, in this sense, reflects aspects of a culture-pattern underlying a vast diversity of religions and cultures. The tendency to absorb within itself so much that is archetypal in nature, crossing religious and cultural boundaries, could be a factor—we dare to suggest—in the Zohar's ultimately ambiguous relationship to that larger world of religious imagination and myth lying beyond the orbits of Jewish monotheistic belief. Midrash and myth meet in the text of the Zohar.

Within its framework of homilies comprising a mystic theosophical commentary on many verses of the Torah, the Zohar contains numerous narrative passages. Many of these are quite fragmentary in nature and serve merely as a narrative framework for the ideational content included in that particular section. Other narratives, however, display considerable literary complexity and power. In the Zohar, the medieval Jewish story acquired wings and reached unprecedented heights. This is the case, even considering the Zohar's own professed denigration of narrative, something the Zohar shared with other voices in the medieval Jewish world.[3]

While the Zohar has been the subject of most impressive research,[4] up to the present time little had been written on the stories found within the text of the Zohar. The tendency in Zohar scholarship has long been, in fact, to minimize the importance of the stories within the Zohar in relation to scholarly concerns and investigations.[5] Currently, however, greater attention is being focused upon the stories as a subject of research, making for a reevaluation of the zoharic story and its importance within the Zohar.[6]

The reader will note that the more complex and developed zoharic stories exemplify significant literary art. This study will take note both of narrative art within the story and the art of the larger homiletic composition in which the story integrates with the nonnarrative content of the homilies. In some cases these stories are multithematic, and different themes are accentuated or alluded to in different elements and on different levels of the narrative. In the zoharic story at its best, the author conveys a multitude of meanings, voices various codes, and utilizes a number of literary and narrative strategies. A fuller understanding of these stories requires a familiarity with the particular complex of symbolism that informs the Zohar. It also requires that the reader listen carefully to the details and nuances of the text, to patterns and interrelationships within the narrative as well as to echoes of older sources mirrored and often significantly transformed in the story.

These stories are the work of a particular author—or group of writers[7]—and to the degree that the stories reflect older narrative traditions and folktale motifs, the author places his indelible stamp upon them. They are marked by a uniqueness of ambiance and of imagery. A zoharic story relates to homiletical, ideational content situated sometimes even within the story itself and is linked in multiple ways with its broader textual context. At the same time, the narrative displays its own nuances and thematics and emphases, having in that sense a life and meaning of its own.

This study of zoharic narrative aims at an in-depth literary analysis of particular stories. Our aim is to illumine the individual story, its meanings and literary power, along with the story's relationship to its larger compositional unit, the zoharic *derush* or homily. These stories have a definite textual context from which they cannot be shorn, and a story's multiple connections on various levels with the larger nonnarrative text are indispensable in defining the meaning of the story itself.

In addition, we shall read these stories with an eye to the insights they might suggest concerning the underlying mindset of the zoharic author, his premises and attitudes and, presumably, those of his circle and his spiritual world. Often the inner narrative logic of a story mirrors basic beliefs and reflects a particular temperament. The stories illumine the zoharic mystic's self-perception, his reflections concerning himself, his situation, and his writing. Sometimes, upon examination, the ultimate subject of a story appears to be the Zohar itself. A zoharic narrative might convey the ephemeral nature of mystic insight—the virtual impossibility of attaining mystic knowledge in this world—and hence the utter preciousness of the mystic truth found in the Zohar. A story might express the alienation of the mystic vis-à-vis both this world and the higher worlds, his sense of being ultimately a stranger to both. It might voice a mindset with which the author could intuitively identify: one distinctly open to imagination, and to the poetic, which infuses its grasp of being. The zoharic stories contain the outlines of a spiritual self-portrait; the author sometimes draws upon and remolds much older motifs to express zoharic wisdom pondering itself, consciously or subconsciously.

A zoharic story, we have already suggested, is not an independent entity. It is rather part of a homily or *derush*, a larger literary unit claiming to reveal the hidden meanings present in a biblical verse. On another level, the individual story is related also to an entire tradition; some of the narratives reflect earlier sources including episodes from biblical literature or from the talmudic-midrashic tradition. The informed reader, the author assumed, was quite aware of the older source obliquely present in the narrative, and the recognition of the source sometimes evokes an implied comparison vital to the meaning of the later story. When a zoharic story recalls a biblical narrative, the tradition of interpretation of that older story becomes an implicit part of the foreground of the zoharic tale as well.

One story of King Solomon found in a strand of zoharic literature, represents a striking example of the retelling of older stories or folk motifs. Each morning, Solomon would ascend upon a large eagle and fly to a place in the dark mountains of the wilderness to learn magic arts. The motif of a magic bird (or carpet) placed at the wise king's service, however, dissolves as Solomon views, on his flight, the place of those who have died in earliest infancy. The theme of magic power thoroughly recedes before a recognition of tragedy as God is overcome with pity for the children who are torn from their families at a tender age, children for whom there is no comfort. Their tears move all the world to weeping (2:112a-113b, *Sava de-mishpatim*). The folk character of an earlier motif has been radically transformed.

One type of intertextuality encountered in the reading of zoharic stories is evident in the profusion of biblical verses quoted in the narrative texts. They lend to the zoharic narrative the qualities of a midrashic story: a story might appear to elucidate a biblical verse; or the latter might appear as a proof text to clinch the implications of the particular story; or a biblical verse—even a single word from a verse—might sometimes serve to evoke or occasion a story. The biblical verses quoted within a zoharic narrative passage are an integral aspect of the story text and often crucially illumine the story.

A biblical verse quoted at the closure of a narrative passage might alter the reader's grasp of the entire story. Sometimes the significance of a quoted verse is evident not in its words but rather in its context within the biblical text, and the zoharic story is implicitly grasped as an overtone of the biblical source. The connection between two seemingly unrelated components of a biblical verse might appear only in light of the idea voiced in a parable. For example, the two apparently unrelated statements located within the same verse, "You are children of the Lord your God; You shall not gash yourselves or shave the front of your heads because of the dead" (Deuteronomy 14:22), are seen as a single idea through the prism of a zoharic parable (1:245b) that explains death as a king calling his son, who had been sent to a village, to return to the royal palace. The villagers lament the departure of the king's son who had lived among them for several years, until one wise man among them explains that the prince's appropriate place is his father's palace. The difficulty in grasping the conjunction of two disparate elements of a biblical verse is resolved when death is understood not as an occasion of grief—with its potentially destructive practices that the Torah prohibits—but rather as one of joy.

Many of the above functions are quite common in classical midrashic texts. But an additional strategy that stands out in the Zohar is the role afforded associations from classical midrashic readings in the use of a biblical verse.

Some significant examples of this function of the quoted biblical verse are clearly evident in the account of the death of Rabbi Simeon bar Yohai, a composition included in the text of the Zohar. The sage's death comes after his disclosure of the most sublime mysteries to the *Idra zuta* (the Small Holy Assembly), seven mystic sages who have survived the death of three of their colleagues in the wake of previous disclosures made during the *Idra rabba* (the Large Holy Assembly) (3:127b-145a). The *Idra zuta* is included in the Zohar's exegesis of the concluding part of Deuteronomy, that includes the death of Moses and the song he recites before his death.

The coffin or bier of Rabbi Simeon, we read there, ascends into the air surrounded by fire, and later enters a burial cave. A voice, heard in the cave uttering praise for the deceased, concludes its words with a quotation from Daniel 12:13: "As for you, go to the end; you shall rest and then rise for your lot at the end of the right hand" (3:296b). Among the midrashic readings of this verse most pertinent to its inclusion in this passage is that found in the *Sifre (Pinhas* 135). There, these words are said to be spoken by God not to Daniel but to Moses, as God tells him, "It is enough for you; you have become very tired; you have worked a great deal. Go and rest, Moses, as is written, 'Go to the end (your end) and you shall rest.' " In other words, Moses is being told: don't seek to enter the land with your people, but be satisfied instead to die and to rest following your labors.

When the bier of Rabbi Simeon rises in the air, a voice is heard inviting all to join in the "wedding feast" of Rabbi Simeon. The voice utters the verse from Isaiah 57:2, "He comes in peace; they shall rest upon their beds." In *Devarim rabbah* 11:10, this verse, too, is related to the death of Moses: "The heavens wept . . . the earth wept . . . . And when Joshua was seeking his master and unable to find him, he also wept." The angels together with Israel then utter the words from Isaiah.

Midrashic readings of a number of verses quoted following the death of the three sages of the Large Holy Assembly—foreshadowing the death of Bar Yohai—similarly recall associations with Moses and his death. After their sudden deaths, the three sages are carried by angels into a canopy spread out above them, where their souls make their departure with a kiss (3:144b), a comment recalling the death of Moses according to a rabbinic tradition (*Devarim rabbah* 11:10).

Three pertinent biblical verses stand out in this passage. Rabbi Simeon refers to himself and his six fellows—the survivors—in quoting the verse from the prophet's vision of the menorah in Zechariah 4:10: "These seven are the eyes of the Lord." Rabbi Abba immediately recalls that six of the lamps of the Temple menorah receive their light from the seventh, Bar Yohai occupying the position of the seventh in the analogy. As the seventh, Bar Yohai is further referred to as "the Sabbath of us all," the one day that blesses the other days of the week and is uniquely holy among them (3:144b).

A comment recorded in *Yalkut shimoni* (2:570) explains the "seven eyes of the Lord" mentioned in Zechariah as "corresponding to the Fathers through Moses," as Moses is the seventh in a list of biblical figures which directly links Abraham with Moses (Abraham, Isaac, Jacob, Levi, Kehat, Amram, Moses).[8] These midrashic overtones of a single verse elucidate three parallel and interconnecting series of seven: the candlelights in the Temple menorah, the seventh day and weekdays, and Moses standing as the pinnacle of the important biblical figures beginning with Abraham.

A discussion in the same zoharic passage, touching on the central role of the seventh day, includes words from Genesis 2:3, "And God blessed the seventh day and hallowed it." The Zohar text again likens Rabbi Simeon bar Yohai to the seventh day, "crowned and hallowed" above the other days of the week (2:145a). And again, the verse connotes a connection, via a midrashic reading in *Vayikra rabbah* 29:11, with Moses; the midrashic passage there explains that all sevenths are favored and that among the Fathers, the seventh was Moses, the favorite in God's eyes.

By evoking midrashic readings, these and other verses create an implicit architectonic network to buttress the Zohar's attribution to Rabbi Simeon bar Yohai the spiritual level and significance of Moses; through it the author portrays the death of Bar Yohai and also of his students as a distinct parallel to the death of Moses.[9]

The same biblical verses relating to the Sabbath are read in midrashic sources in a way which accentuates the joyous character of the seventh day (*Bereshit rabbati*, 35), likens it to a wedding (*Pesikta rabbati*, 35), and stresses the prohibition of mourning on that day (*Bereshit rabbah* 100:7; 11:1). The various overtones interweave: Rabbi Simeon is likened to the seventh day on which there is no mourning; hence his death should be regarded as an occasion not of mourning but of joy. Also like the seventh day, the death of Rabbi Simeon is described in terms of a wedding feast (3:296b): with the death of such a person, the culmination and total effect of his life, his deeds, and his mystical insights effect a divine wedding in the higher worlds, a union between masculine and feminine powers within the Godhead. We have observed here that a biblical verse quoted in a zoharic story can allude at the same time to multiple midrashic readings, all of which are relevant to the network of meanings of the zoharic narrative.

From this example, we note that it is sometimes on the level of associations culled from midrashic readings of a biblical verse that the particular verse relates most closely and compactly to the zoharic story. Not only did the author read a biblical text to a large extent through the lens of its midrashic interpretations, but the intertextual strategy of such associations comprises a significant aspect of the subtle and complex literary art of the Zohar.

While midrash in its classical form ultimately sought to make explicit what was felt to be implicit in the biblical text, in the zoharic story a quoted verse often alludes to a meaning without necessarily voicing it explicitly. The ultimate significance of a quoted biblical verse in a zoharic story might be located in its overtones and hence remains on the level of allusion. At this level, the zoharic art of biblical quotation belongs to the realm of the poetic.

Even the more complex zoharic stories are not set apart in any clear way from the text surrounding them. Consequently, though a narrative can be grasped in terms of its story pattern, it can still lack a clearly defined beginning or concluding point within the larger text. The story appears to merge with its landscape and with the texture of its context, with what precedes and follows, without any sharp lines of demarcation. A story might relate either explicitly or more subtly to any point in the larger homiletic text in which it is located. Consequently its background, though distinctly nonnarrative in nature, is often integral to the body of the story.

For example: in a passage interpreting the verse which states that Moses "came to Horeb, the mountain of God" (Exodus 3:1), the question is raised: How was Moses able to identify the mountain? It is explained first that birds flew in the air encompassing the mountain with wings outstretched but never flying over the mountain. It is then mentioned that Moses noticed birds flying toward him from the direction of the mountain and falling at his feet. Realizing the special character of the mountain, he led his flock of sheep to a point in the distance and proceeded to ascend the mountain alone (2:21a). The motif of the birds directing him to the mountain site in one way or another echoes the subject of birds earlier in the zoharic discussion of the same Torah portion. There the text mentions that both birds' wings and children might proclaim an imminent change in political power decreed first in the other world (2:6b). The Messiah's conceal-ment in the chamber known as the "Bird's Nest" (2:7b; 8b) is also mentioned, and the name is explained in that the Shekhinah, the aspect of the Godhead closest to our world and experience, is said to fly about Paradise each day (2:8a). The forces of the Messiah will be strengthened, we then read, by schoolchildren, young scholars likened to *efroḥim* ("fledglings" or "young birds," 2:9a). The story, it becomes apparent, echoes an image or motif still fresh in the reader's, and the author's, mind.

In a more complex example, many different strands—diverse themes, motifs, and concepts—might reverberate together in a single story. One cannot grasp the narrative art of any particular zoharic story without observing the relation of the story to the larger homiletic composition, or even to the series of such homilies in which it is situated. For reasons of compactness, the translations in this vol-ume are generally limited to the narrative content itself, with only a paraphrase of closely related homiletic content located within the nar-rative passage; in the commentary following the story, how-ever, we will attempt to elucidate the connections of the story with the larger homiletic text, connections with elements that might either precede, be situated within, or follow the story.

Another essential characteristic observed in certain zoharic stories is a distinct tendency to encompass within a story the totality of history, even the totality of cosmic history as grasped by Kabbalah. A single story or parable sometimes represents a vast canvas that includes all of time from the very beginning of things until the hour of redemption, much as contemporary astronomers have produced a drawer-size map of the entire physical universe!

As an example, let us refer to one such narrative passage that connects several strands in a way to comprise the totality of human history. A zoharic story (3:19a) relates that Lilith, the female personification of the evil, demonic forces, cohabited with Adam before his body received a soul. Then when Adam's body, containing both its male and female sides, received a soul, his female self was fashioned into Eve, whom God brought to Adam "like a bride to the canopy." Lilith fled to the cities of the coast, where she remains to the present time. There, from the seacoast—suggesting the boundary between order and chaos—Lilith attempts to entice Adam's descendents. The time of enticements and human failures is equated with the span of human history, and the passage then leaps to what will follow when God will destroy Rome and will proceed to settle Lilith there among its ruins "as she is the ruin of the world." The destruction and ruins of Jerusalem are mirrored inversely in this apocalyptic event, the devastation of Rome, the city which symbolizes the power that so oppressed Israel and had destroyed Jerusalem.

The span of time encompassed in this brief story concerning Lilith extends from before Adam received a soul to the redemptive righting of the wrongs of history, from the very beginning to the very end of the human story. The story leaps, however, from the beginning to the time of redemption with only implied mention of the intervening historical time as a span in which Lilith entices humankind to sin.

Another example of this type of story encompassing an entire history is the zoharic parable of a king angered by the behavior of his beloved only son (2:189a). The king strikes the son but then forgives him. When the son persists in his notorious behavior, the father drives him from the house, and the son, away from the palace, turns to a decidedly immoral life.[10] In response to the queen's weeping, the king offers to restore him to the palace in a manner eliciting no attention—in keeping with the king's honor, which was shamed by his son's conduct—and gives the queen full responsibility for him. Once again the son sins, and this time his father expels both the son and his mother—for if mother and son are to suffer together, the king knows that his son will repent.

If the allusions are not sufficiently transparent, the text that follows explains the parable as referring to Egyptian bondage, the Babylonian exile, the return from that exile without any fanfare similar to the miracle at the Sea of Reeds, and the later exile at the hands of Rome. While the allusions chronologically terminate at that point, the king's intent implies also the redemption to come. The entire history of Israel is encapsulated in this brief parable of a king, his son, and the son's mother. At the same time, the parable's allusions interpret the happenings of Israel's history through reference to another dimension of being. Interwoven with historical experience is the drama of the exile of the Shekhinah, separated from the masculine powers within the realm of divinity. Human sin is viewed as a cause of displacement both within human history and within the higher levels of being. This parable is one of a series of parables, found in different places within the Zohar, which speak of the interrelationships of a king, his wife, and their son, and of one relationship affecting another within this triad.

The context of this parable is the apparent contradiction between the biblical promises to Israel and Israel's historical reality as a small and subject people.[11] The inner dialectic of the parable, however, points to a larger apparent contradiction between the judgment Israel has experienced in its exile and divine compassion.

Focusing upon this same parable more closely, the reader notes two contrasting tendencies: one making for distance and remoteness, the other making for nearness and presence. The former exemplifies the father who decrees exile for his son and who, while initially saddened, does not succumb to weeping for him. The latter tendency exemplifies the mother ceaselessly weeping and pleading for her exiled son. That very polarity, however, is transcended: the former tendency—making for distance, remoteness, and exile—is ultimately designed to achieve a state of true closeness between father and son.

The son's mother is exiled in order to ensure their reunion as a
family; exile is decreed for the purpose of annihilating the roots of
exile in the son's behavioral pattern, his propensity to sin. Behind the
face of harsh judgment the parable perceives divine compassion.

The turning point in the parable is the exile of the prince's
mother, which concludes the story. What follows is the stating of an
expectation and intent; the son's repentance and restoration to the
palace is merely implied. But what is implied, nevertheless, comprises
part of the total pattern of the story, the totality of history it signifies.
The implied redemption and restoration serve, in fact, as the more
decisive turning point, even though they lie beyond the sequence of
events comprising the "story" as told. The story's extension to
redemption, even by implication, is most significant in illuminating
both its character and the actual canvas of time it reflects.

The passage is also interesting in other respects—if we can digress
for a moment. This type of parable, in which the figure representing
the Shekhinah pleads for compassion for her children in the face of
the father's inclination toward strict justice, finds an interesting parallel in the role of the Virgin Mary in Christian lore and legend of thirteenth-century Spain.[12] Mary was thought not only to have greater
sympathy for human pain and misfortune but also to protect those
who turned to her from the legitimate wrath of a just God. She
offered a mother's protection while seeking to assuage the father's
anger. It is interesting that the height of the cult of the Virgin Mary,
both as a popular phenomenon and in literary expression, occurred in
Spain precisely in the late twelfth and thirteenth centuries.[13] The parallel roles of the Shekhinah and Mary in this respect might point to
the significance of a shared landscape in which very different religious
traditions lived and evolved in medieval Spain. The parallels between
the Shekhinah and Mary, notwithstanding of course obvious and
essential differences, might also include shared elements in the symbolism of the two. Both the rose and the garden symbolize the
Shekhinah in the Zohar; Mary, too, is specifically identified with roses
and gardens, and her association as a *rosa mystica* accounts for the
term "rosary," prayer beads used when Catholics pray to Mary.[14] In
examining the stories in this collection we will occasionally note other
parallels suggesting the effect of a common landscape, one reflected
both in the Zohar and in the emerging Spanish literature of the same

period. But let us return to our basic idea at this point.

In his book *Anatomy of Criticism*, the noted critic Northrop Frye speaks of the encyclopedic form, consisting often of collections of tales, myths, epics, and chronicles that join together to form aggregates. Those aggregates represent, according to Frye, a totality of time and experience extending from creation to apocalypse. The Bible, for Frye, exemplifies this kind of encyclopedic structure, a total myth culminating with a redeemed world. In different modes, various kinds of literary works serve as analogues to the Bible in this respect and exemplify, in their own terms, its encyclopedic quality and character, built around five basic events: "creation, fall, exile, redemption, and restoration."[15]

Considered as a literary work, the Zohar exemplifies this encyclopedic character. A sense of the totality of time and experience pervades the Zohar, even though the Zohar does not express this sense in any systematic or chronological arrangement. The Zohar, indeed, reflects a much vaster canvas than does the Bible; it begins not with the creation of our universe but rather with the initial stirring within the *Ein sof*, within infinite divine being. That stirring effected a chain of development accounting ultimately for both the emanation of the divine personality, the sefirotic world, and the coming into being of this physical world.

In the Zohar, that encyclopedic canvas, the totality of time encompassing the entire scope of human history from creation to redemption, is sometimes refracted in individual narratives. The encyclopedic story in the Zohar recalls also another phenomenon recurrent in the same work. Several of the homilies comprising the Zohar conclude with a redemptive closure. In various midrashic works of an earlier period, a homily concludes with a messianic closure that speaks of redemption on a national and historic level; the Zohar's homilies sometimes both echo and transcend that kind of messianic closure by ending with a note of redemption on a cosmic level. This type of concluding note refers to the time when God and His Name will be one and when death, along with the evil impulse and the impure forces, will be vanquished forever.[16] When the perspective voiced in such a redemptive closure is given narrative content, the result is an encyclopedic story.

More often, the encyclopedic quality radiates from other narratives in the Zohar constructed upon a much more limited time frame but nevertheless presupposing and alluding to a larger, total story and to the conflict that permeates it. We note, for example, an account of the desert dweller, (2:183b-187b), a rather marginal story in terms of its narrative qualities; yet this same account conveys an infinitely larger story stretching from the triumph of the evil forces, a consequence of the making of the Golden Calf, to the implied point of redemptive time in the future. In that redemptive moment, the evil forces will be removed as a consequence of the mystic activity of the sage residing in the desert, the scene of darkness. An almost hermitlike sage seeks to negate that triumph of the *Sitra ahra*, the demonic and impure forces, at an earlier hour of history.

The stories constructed around either a supernatural postponement of death ("Death Postponed") or the revival of a person already dead ("A Child's Tears and His Father's Resurrection") mirror the concept of resurrection associated with the time of redemption following the culmination of history. Narrative events in these stories are patterned to reflect eschatological events. It is interesting to compare the pagan sacred story, in which the equivalent of resurrection occurs at the mythic beginning of things, the Christian sacred story in which it occurs at a point of time within the continuum of history, and the Jewish sacred story, exemplified in the Zohar, in which resurrection and the elimination of death are located in the future as the climax and culmination of history.

Frye's association of the encyclopedic—as a total myth or sacred story encompassing all of time—with a body of Scripture is highly suggestive. For the encyclopedic quality, represented in some of these stories, might comprise a key element in the Zohar's acceptance within the world of Kabbalah, in effect, as a canonical text.

Over five hundred years after the Zohar was written, a similar grasp of total experience in narrative form marks the tales of Rabbi Nahman of Bratzlav.[17] On one level these tales—which also draw upon the Zohar's world of imagery—portray a history of the cosmos in terms of the world view of Lurianic Kabbalah, a later stage in the history of Jewish mysticism; they mirror the conception of a history extending from the initial act of a contraction within the infinite divine being through cosmic catastrophe to a future redemption, a mending of the estrangement and exile at the heart of being. That sense of totality, an all-encompassing sacred story in Frye's sense, might be crucial in explaining why those tales of Rabbi Nahman came to be regarded by his followers on a par, virtually, with Scripture.

Having voiced these comments and suggestions concerning the textual character of the zoharic story and its explicit or implicit encyclopedic nature, our attention henceforth will be given to a number of specific narratives contained in the text of the Zohar. And while a literary study of any aspect of the Zohar is inherently undertaken with a certain degree of trepidation, we proceed, even considering the potential pitfalls, with the hope that this collection of studies might contribute to an enhanced appreciation of some of the narratives representing perhaps the very summit of the medieval Jewish story.

Notes

1. Gershom Scholem, *Major Trends in Jewish Mysticism*, 186-204. Note also the discussion of Moses de Leon in Daniel Matt, *Zohar—The Book of Enlightenment*, 3-10. The nineteenth-century historian Heinrich Graetz had identified Moses de Leon as the author of the Zohar (*History of the Jews*, 3:11-24.) Much more recently, Moshe Idel (*Kabbalah: New Perspectives*, 119), subtly questions Moses de Leon's authorship of the Zohar by contrasting aspects of the Zohar with concepts in Moses de Leon's Hebrew writings. As an inquiry concerning the authorship of the Zohar is not within the boundaries of this study, we shall refer to the writer simply as "the zoharic author."

2. Heinrich Graetz, *History of the Jews*, 5:121.

3. Harry Sperling and Maurice Simon, trans., *The Zohar* 3:149a-b; 152a. The author of the Zohar, for example, viewed the Toraitic narrative as the surface dimension of the Torah, one likened to a mere garment concealing the Torah's mystic essence. See Joseph Dan, *Hasippur ha'ivri bimei habeinayim*, 7-12. The professed deflation of narrative in these passages might actually be somewhat deceiving, as they nonetheless affirm the capacity of story to serve as a garment of ultimate truth. While the philosophical strain in Spanish-Jewish culture, highly abstract in character, was critical of and even embarrassed by aggadah, i.e., the traditions of Jewish lore, including its

narrative expressions, hardly appropriate to a systematic, coherent, and rational world view, the Zohar represents a rebirth of aggadah and its undisciplined imagination.

4. The basic findings are summarized in Scholem, *Major Trends*, lectures 5 and 6, and Isaiah Tishby, introduction to *Mishnat hazohar*.

5. Scholem, *Major Trends*, 171-172; Tishby, *Mishnat hazohar* 1:25-28; and *Dan, Hasippur ha'ivri*, 32.

6. Matti Megged (*Ha'or hanehshakh*) opened up the subject of the story and esthetics in the Zohar, although his work on the subject is in the nature of an overview and, for our purposes, lacks in-depth analysis of particular stories as well as the kinds of conclusions that can emerge from such analysis. Yehuda Leibes ("*Hamashiah shel hazohar*," 103-4) has written on the ideological significance of narrative in the Zohar. More recently Michele Oron ("*Kol haneshamah tehalel yah*" and "*Me'omanut haderush shel ba'al hazohar*") and Noami Teneh, doctoral student at Bar-Ilan University, are examining the zoharic stories in terms of literary qualities and structure. Note also Mordecai Pechter's study of the integration of narrative and homily in the Zohar ("*Bein layla levoker*").

7. Leibes ("*Ketsad nithaber sefer hazohar*,") has suggested that a circle of students worked together with Moses de Leon in composing the Zohar.

8. This list appears in other connections in midrashic sources. See *Pesikta derav kahana*, 155a.

9. See Leibes, "*Hamashiah shel hazohar*," 105-7, 205.

10. The sins of the son at this point in the parable might reflect criticism of the milieu and way of life of the Jewish courtier class in medieval Spain.

11. This contradiction proved to be deeply disturbing at critical points in the history of Spanish Jewry. See Yitzhak Baer, *A History of the Jews in Christian Spain* 1:75-76, 330.

12. In *Las Cantigas* 14, written at the court of Alfonso X, El Sabio, for example, St. Peter pleads with Mary to request forgiveness for the soul of a wayward monk who, during his lifetime, had displayed marked devotion to her. God accedes to the pleading of Mary and restores the monk to life for a second chance. (See Frank Callcott, *The Supernatural in Early Spanish Literature*, 32.) A similar pattern can be observed in Berceo's *Milagros de Nuestra Sénora* 7, among other medieval Spanish tales. See John Eston Keller, *Pious Brief Narrative in Medieval Castilian and Galician Verse*, 33; Keller, *Gonzalo de Berceo*, 139; and Sondra Rosyla Heller, *Characterization of the Virgin Mary in Four Thirteenth-Century Narrative Collections of Miracles*, 100-103, who points out that those tales of Berceo accentuate not the sinner's repentance and remorse but rather the goodness of Mary. Reluctant to appeal to God or Christ, the sinner can depend upon Mary, who never castigates, to convince Christ to forgive the sinner.

13. Colbert I. Nepaulsingh (*Toward a History of Literary Composition in Medieval Spain*, 29-30, 226-27, 229-30) makes the claim that the cult of the

Virgin Mary is significant in the epic of the Cid and was dominant in the thirteenth century and its literature. See also Heller (*Characterization of the Virgin Mary*, 3) who points out that this kind of role, actually unorthodox in terms of the official position of the Church, came to the fore in the twelfth and thirteenth centuries.

14. Nepaulsingh, *Toward a History*, 19, 34, 35. Also see Eitone Wilkins, *The Rose-garden Game: The Symbolic Background to the European Prayerbeads.* Among such parallels between the Shekhinah in the Zohar and the role of Mary prominent in popular Christian culture during roughly the same period, one can point to Jewish and Christian exegesis of the Song of Songs. Beginning in the twelfth century, Christian exegetes interpreted this biblical text in reference to Mary (See Ann Astell, *Song of Songs in the Middle Ages*, 15-16, 42-50, 60-72), while the kabbalistic reading of the same text focused upon the Shekhinah and her relationship with the other aspects of the Godhead. Similarly, the Shekhinah, in zoharic symbolism, served as a supernal model of the people of Israel, while Catholic exegesis came to regard Mary as a model of the Church (Astell, 62-63, and notes to those pages). For the association of the color red and the rose with Mary, see Heller, 140, 145.

15. Northrop Frye, *Anatomy of Criticism*, 315, 317.

16. While Maimonides, representing the rational philosophical tradition, deflated the messianic hope and defined it basically in political terms as the end of foreign subjugation of Jewry (*Mishnah torah, hilkhot teshuvah*, end of chap. 9), the Zohar, in contrast, described the messianic fulfillment as a radical change in the very nature of the world. See Yitzhak Baer, *A History of the Jews in Christian Spain*, 1:249.

17. Nahman ben Simhah of Bratzlav, "*Sefer sippure hama'asiyot*," Trans. Arnold J. Band *Nahman of Bratslav: The Tales.*

The Upper Sefirot of Keter, Crown; Ḥokhmah,
Wisdom; and Binah, Understanding.

Grief, Triumph, Expulsion

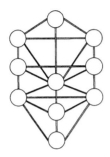

A student's grief over Simeon Bar Yohai's death gives way to a vision of the sage in the Celestial Academy, followed in turn by the disciple's expulsion from the very setting of the vision.

Rabbi Hiyya bent down to the ground and bowed, kissing the dust and weeping. He cried out, "Dust, dust, how utterly stubborn you are! How brazen you are, that in you all the delights of the eye wear out in a state of oblivion. All the pillars of light in the world you extinguish and shatter. Indeed, how very brazen are you! For the Holy Light that illumined the world, the great master through whose merit the world continues to exist, decays and wears away within you.

"Rabbi Simeon, the very light of light, the light of the worlds—you perish in the dust, you who are responsible for sustaining the world."

Completely beside himself for a moment, he exclaimed, "Dust, dust, be not proud, for the Pillars of the world[1] will not be delivered into your hands; Rabbi Simeon will not wear away in you."

Still weeping, Rabbi Hiyya stood up and began walking together with Rabbi Yose. Beginning that day, he fasted for a total of forty days[2] with the hope of being able to see Rabbi Simeon (in a vision). But instead, he was told, "You are not permitted to see him." He wept[3] and fasted another forty days; then, in a vision, he saw Rabbi Simeon with his son, Rabbi Eleazar, with thousands listening to his words, as they were conversing on the very subject on which Rabbi Yose himself had just spoken.[4] He noticed many large winged heaven-

19

ly beings upon whose wings Rabbi Simeon and his son, Rabbi Eleazar, rose upward to the celestial academy of the heavenly firmament where those winged angels proceeded to wait for them. He perceived that the sages appeared brighter and brighter until their light was even more dazzling than that of the sun.

Rabbi Simeon then announced, "Let Rabbi Hiyya enter and observe how the Holy One, blessed be He, will, in the future, renew the countenance of the righteous. Blessed is the one who has entered here without disgrace, and blessed is the one who, in that other world, stands as a Pillar of spiritual strength."

Rabbi Hiyya saw himself enter, as Rabbi Simeon rose up together with all the other Pillars who had been seated there. Embarrassed at this mark of honor accorded him, he immediately seated himself at the feet of Rabbi Simeon. A voice was heard, "Lower your eyes, and neither raise your head nor gaze."[5] Looking downward, he sensed a bright light over in the distance. He again heard the same voice, which now uttered, "You celestial ones, hidden, concealed, those with open eyes, those who roam throughout the world, gaze and observe. And you who are below, asleep, with eyes closed tight, awaken! Who among you, before your coming here, had transformed darkness into light, the bitter into the sweet?[6] Who among you had waited daily for that light which appears at the hour when the King remembers the Gazelle,[7] and brings Her out of Exile, when He is majestically glorified and all the kings of the world address him as King? Whoever does not wait with such longing every day while in that other world can have no place here."

Meanwhile, he noted several of the *haverim*,[8] all those mighty Pillars, gathering around, and he observed that they were lifted up to the Heavenly Academy. They were ascending, while others were descending. And he saw the angel who came and swore that from behind the veil[9] he had heard that each day the King remembers and visits the Gazelle, who is lying in the dust. At that moment, the King strikes all three hundred and ninety[10] firmaments, which then all tremble and shake before His presence. Tears[11] as hot as fire well up in His eyes and fall into the Great Sea. From those tears the Master of the Sea emerges, the one who, hallowing the Name of the Holy One, agrees to swallow all the waters of Creation. He will absorb them within himself at the very time that all the nations will gather against the holy people, so that the waters might part and the people pass through on dry land.[12]

He then heard a voice calling, "Make way, make way, for King-Messiah is coming to the Academy of Rabbi Simeon." All the righteous ones there were heads of renowned academies of learning, and all the *haverim* of each of those academies made their way upward to the Heavenly Academy. The Messiah came to all those academies and placed his stamp of approval upon the learning and interpretations taught by those sages. And at that hour the Messiah himself appeared, wearing celestial crowns, gifts from the heads of the academies. All the *haverim* then rose up together with Rabbi Simeon, whose light now ascended aloft and extended to the very heights of the firmament. The Messiah said to him, "My master, you are indeed blessed, for your Torah[13] has risen upward in the form of three hundred and seventy lights,[14] each light dividing into six hundred and thirteen[15] shades of persimmon. And the Holy One, blessed be He, places His approval on the Torah taught in your academy and also in that of Hezekiah, king of Judah,[16] and in that of Ahiyah Hashiloni.[17] I myself have not come to approve the Torah of your academy, but the presiding angel has come here, and I know that he will not enter into any other academy but yours."

At that very hour, Rabbi Simeon told him what he had heard under oath from the angel. Immediately the Messiah, totally agitated, raised his voice, causing the firmaments to tremble along with the Great Sea and Leviathan too, and the foundations of the world were beginning to shake.

While all this was happening, the Messiah noticed Rabbi Hiyya seated at the feet of Rabbi Simeon. He asked, "Who brought here one who is still clad in a garment of that other world?"[18]

Rabbi Simeon explained, "It is Rabbi Hiyya, the light of the lamp of Torah."

The Messiah told him, "In that case, let him and his sons undergo death ('be gathered in')[19] and be accepted as members of your academy."

At this, Rabbi Simeon requested, "Grant him time before that occurs."

And so time was granted to him and he departed trembling, tears falling from his eyes. Shaking and weeping, Rabbi Hiyya said, "Truly blessed is the portion of the righteous in that world, and especially blessed is the portion of bar Yohai. Concerning just that kind of reward it is written, 'I endow those who love me with substance; I will fill their treasures'" (Proverbs 8:21).[20]

(1:4ab)

Notes

1. Scholars of Torah who are likened to pillars upholding the universe (Berakhot 28b).
2. Baba Metsiah 85a mentions the practice of fasting for a period of forty days. According to the Torah, Moses, upon Mount Sinai, neither ate nor drank for that period of time (Exodus 34:28). A source in *Kohelet rabbah* on Ecclesiastes 9:10 speaks of fasting for the purpose of seeing, in a dream, a sage who had died.
3. Moshe Idel, in *Kabbalah: New Perspectives*, 77-88, has traced examples of self-induced weeping as a mystical practice in order to obtain a vision or dream. This practice, Idel points out, is sometimes connected with visiting a gravesite, an association of direct relevance to the setting of the first part of this narrative.
4. The mystic significance of the first two words of the Torah as discussed by Rabbi Yose (1:3b). The discussion of the very same subject in the heavenly academy is the direct link between this account and its textual context.
5. Only those who had died an earthly death were capable of beholding the great light in all its brightness.
6. Through their deeds, they have transformed judgment into mercy (Abraham Galante, *Zohare hamah*, [a commentary on the Zohar]).
7. The Shekhinah (the tenth and lowest of the *Sefirot*, forms of divine being and energy that emanated from the infinite state of the Godhead).
8. "Fellows," members of a circle of students of mystic teaching.
9. The veil, *pargod*, surrounding the divine throne. From behind the *pargod* one can hear secrets not known beyond that supernal space. See Hagigah 15a.
10. The number of firmaments (2:195b). The letters of the word *shamayim* (heavens) have the combined numerical value of 390.
11. The tears (see Zohar 2:9a, 19b, 195b; 3:172b, the motif based on Berakhot 59a) represent the qualities of judgment, which, when they fall into

the Sea (a symbol of the sefirah, *Malkhut*, the Shekhinah), sweeten its waters, tempering judgment or even transforming judgment into mercy (Galante, *Zohare ḥamah*, and Jacob Moses Safrin, *Damasek eliezer*, based on Zohar 2:172a).

12. Reference to the splitting of the *yam suf* (Reed Sea) after the Exodus from Egypt (Exodus 14:21-22), the miraculous occurrence regarded as the prototype of the redemption to come (Isaiah 11:15).

13. The substance of his teaching.

14. The figure three hundred represents the first three *Sefirot*, with seventy signifying the lower seven *Sefirot* that emanated from them (Galante, *Zohare ḥamah*).

15. The number that represents the sum of the *mitzvot* (commandments) found in the Torah and also of the limbs and sinews of the human body.

16. King of Judah during the latter part of the eighth century B.C.E. In later Jewish tradition he is portrayed as a righteous and devout ruler who, devoted to the study of Torah, promoted the study of the Torah tradition (*Shir hashirim rabbah* 4:8; Sanhedrin 94b). According to Sanhedrin 99a, Hezekiah is a messianic figure; see Yehuda Leibes, *Hamashiah shel hazohar*, 92).

17. A biblical prophet from the period preceding the literary prophets. He lived during the reign of Solomon and played a role in political affairs after Solomon's death. In kabbalistic lore, he is portrayed as a teacher of mystic tradition.

18. The physical body and the accompanying mental faculties and psychological makeup associated with and dependent upon the body.

19. Literally, "be gathered in." "To be gathered to one's people" is a biblical expression for death (Genesis 25:8; 35:29; 49:22, 29).

20. Referring to treasures of wisdom (Moses Cordovero, *Or hayakar*). Chapter 8 of Proverbs is devoted in its entirety to the importance of words of wisdom and to the reward for fulfilling them. In later sources, the verse is understood as relating to the reward of the righteous in the World-to-Come (See Mishnah Oktsin 3:12). In *Pesikta derav kahana* 200b, the verse refers to Moses' reward following his death. Elsewhere in the Zohar (1:242b), the verse is understood as the World-to-Come. It is also specified in the Zohar (2:166b) that the verse suggests the three hundred and ten (numerical value of *yesh*, "substance") worlds that God has prepared for the delight of the righteous in the World-to-Come (also *Yalkut shimoni* 1:20, based on Sanhedrin 100a).

Note: This story from the Zohar was later recreated in a legend told about the Baal Shem Tov, one that invites comparison with the zoharic source. The hasidic legend appears in Jacob and Israel Berger, *Ataret ya'akov veyisra'el*, 53-54, with the claim that it was copied from an old letter dated 1798-1799. A partial English translation of that hasidic legend is found in Abraham Joshua Heschel, *The Circle of the Baal Shem Tov: Studies in Hasidism*, ed. Samuel H. Dresner, 144-145.

Commentary

The wondrous nature of the teachings of Rabbi Simeon bar Yohai relating to the opening word of the Torah evokes the telling of this story. The story conveys the response to the master's death of Rabbi Hiyya, one of his fellows and students. It is occasioned, more directly, by report of a discussion in the Heavenly Academy, of a point made by one of the mystic sages in the preceding discourse, close to the very beginning of the Zohar. The story, which interrupts the flow of the discourse in the text, also deepens the sense of awe concerning these same discursive teachings. Going beyond both eulogy and elegy, the narrative account is a lofty evaluation of the words and teachings of the master, Rabbi Simeon bar Yohai, the talmudic sage whom the Zohar claims to be the human channel and authority of its teachings.

The narrative passes through three distinct emotional states: first, grief; then, vision and exultation, and finally, trembling. A clear turning point both signals and causes the movement from one emotion to another. And yet as different as those states are in character, certain threads connect and echo from one section to another, making for a cohesiveness in the account as a whole.

First comes the elegiac opening. This section, depicting the aftermath of the death of bar Yohai, strikes a note both of deep grief and a depth of humility, as Rabbi Hiyya kisses the dust in response to his teacher's death. This act, in addition, also connotes "death by means

24

of a kiss," a dying that transcends or avoids the bitter nature and experience of death as we know it. While in Jewish tradition this kind of death is associated primarily with that of Moses,[1] in the Zohar it is associated also with bar Yohai and with three of his students who similarly die in a state of a total cleaving to God (Zohar 3:144b). Bending *down* to kiss the dust, Rabbi Hiyya is transported *upward* in a visionary ascent to the Heavenly Academy.

That opening passage, so elegiac in character, is both a response to the death of bar Yohai and a broader statement on the nature of death. This outpouring of emotion is a reflection of distinct literary power. Death is described as the triumph of dust over all else, including all that the eye can see and all in which it takes delight.

The narrative, at this point, echoes a motif in a talmudic legend told about Alexander of Macedon. In that *aggadah*, the conquering ruler, coming to the very door of Paradise, demands a gift and is given an eyeball. The king proceeds to weigh all his precious metals together but amazingly they fail to outweigh that small eyeball. The sages, when asked, explain to him that the eyeball of a human being, by nature, is never satisfied (Proverbs 27:20; Ecclesiastes 4:8). Asked for proof, the sages place over the eyeball a little dust, signifying death, and immediately the gold and silver outweighs the eyeball.[2]

Bar Yohai is described in terms of light; but with death the light is consumed, leaving only darkness in its place. We recall the meaning of the word Zohar itself as "light, brightness, splendor." In an elegiac story relating to the death of Rabbi Eleazar the Great found in an earlier stratum of the Zohar, *Midrash hane'elam*, Rabbi Akiva, hearing word of the sage's death, tore his clothing and cried, "Heavens, heavens, tell the sun and the moon that the light which was greater than they has become darkened" (1:99a).

After the elegiac opening, Rabbi Hiyya's frame of mind changes as he defiantly denies the right of death to have such effect. Refuting that power of death, he cried out: "Dust, dust, be not proud," words that distinctly recall to the modern reader those of the English poet John Donne.[3]

With this transformation of mood, the first of the two turning points in the passage, Rabbi Hiyya's wish is granted and he receives a vision of bar Yohai with his son in the Heavenly Academy, where deceased scholars study after death. Whereas darkness holds sway in

this world, the Heavenly Academy is depicted in terms of total lumi-
nation. The triumph of dust, of death below, is now blotted out by
the radiance that dominates the scene. The eye clearly triumphs over
the dust, not the other way around as in the preceding elegiac statement. This scene, moreover, is one of virtually total brightness; it is a
kind of beatific vision in narrative, reflecting the very name of the
Zohar.

What redeems the passage from complete monotony in its brilliant, unmarred brightness is the Exile of the Shekhinah, mentioned
twice within the following section of this episode. Within that very
scene marked by seemingly total brightness, the reader is informed, as
a divine secret disclosed from behind the heavenly veil, that God
recalls the Shekhinah (the Divine Presence, "Gazelle"), trodden in
the dust, and weeps. The Shekhinah is also called *knesset yisra'el*, "the
assembly of Israel," and symbolizes the people, Israel, similarly exiled
and trodden. God's weeping echoes that of Rabbi Hiyya at the story's
opening, prior to his vision of bar Yohai in the Heavenly Academy,
just as the dust in which the Shekhinah is trodden recalls Rabbi
Hiyya's kissing the dust in his state of grief.

The sorrowful divine secret serves as a very precise narrative connection. God weeps, and the Messiah, hearing the divine weeping,
vents his anger. And it is within that expression of his anger that the
Messiah takes note of Rabbi Hiyya, a person of this world who is
present there in the scene of the Heavenly Academy; the Messiah's
anger colors his questioning of Rabbi Hiyya. And it is Rabbi Simeon
bar Yohai who assuages that anger on the part of the Messiah, which
is now directed toward the former's student.

As a dream-vision in which Rabbi Hiyya is the beholder and
dreamer, the vision ultimately illumines not the destiny and lot of
Rabbi Simeon but rather that of Rabbi Hiyya and represents the exis-
tential condition of the mystic in this world.

The Messiah takes note of Rabbi Hiyya as "still clad in the garments of that other world," garments consisting of a physical body
and of those levels of the soul that relate to a material existence.
When Rabbi Simeon refers to the high level of Rabbi Hiyya and of
his teachings, the Messiah responds by offering to make Rabbi Hiyya
and his sons official members of the Heavenly Academy. "Let them
be gathered," he says, the latter verb connoting death (see note 18,

page 23). Acceptance would necessarily involve his proceeding through the passageway of death, since the experience of the higher world is not for those who still belong to this world. During the course of the narrative, the focus has shifted from the death of Rabbi Simeon to Rabbi Hiyya's own death, which is postponed; only later upon his death—in its own time—will Rabbi Hiyya be able to enter as a member of the Heavenly Academy.

Rabbi Simeon's earlier order allowing Rabbi Hiyya to enter is seen, in retrospect, to be highly problematic as even he lacks that authority. And the Messiah's condition for Hiyya's remaining in the Heavenly Academy recalls, in part, the mood of the earlier announcement to Rabbi Hiyya following his first forty-day fast, "You are not permitted. . . ."

The narrative recalls a number of talmudic passages. The association of Rabbi Hiyya with the scene of the Heavenly Academy might well stem from a story in which Elijah warns a sage that though he might see the chariots of the departed scholars as they ascend to the Heavenly Academy, he should not look at the carriage of Rabbi Hiyya, for its brightness will blind him. Elijah, in the talmudic passage, explained furthermore that while other carriages are accompanied by angels, that of Rabbi Hiyya has no need of angels to direct its movements.[4]

The Messiah's reaction to the presence of Rabbi Hiyya in the Heavenly Academy recalls another talmudic legend[5] in which the angels reacted similarly to Moses when he ascended to the upper world to receive the Torah. "What is one born of woman doing among us?" In that aggadah, attributed to Rabbi Joshua ben Levi, God then ordered Moses to justify to the angels His giving the infinitely precious Torah to flesh and blood.

Our story recalls, in addition, another talmudic legend told about the same Rabbi Joshua ben Levi. Just before the time of death designated for him, it is told, the Angel of Death was ordered first to grant whatever wishes the sage might request. When approached by the Angel of Death, Rabbi Joshua ben Levi requested to see his place in the other world. When the Angel of Death consented, the sage requested in addition that the Angel of Death give him his knife so that he would not be frightened along the way; this too was granted. Arriving in Paradise, the sage, noting his place, jumped over the wall into the Garden of Eden and swore to the Angel of Death that he would not return. Only upon a command uttered by a heavenly voice (*bat-kol*) did Rabbi Joshua ben Levi return the knife to the Angel of Death, who needed it to fulfill his required tasks. Elijah, the legend continues, greeted the sage, announcing, "Make room for the son of Levi," who—interestingly for our purposes—then found Rabbi Simeon bar Yohai in Paradise seated upon thirteen tables (or stools) of pure gold.[6]

Another talmudic legend[7] tells of the Babylonian scholar, Rabbah ben Nahamani, an authority on laws relating to the skin affliction *tsara'at*, who was called to the Heavenly Academy to decide a particular case about which the Holy One, blessed be He, and the sages could not agree. Upon being called to the Academy, Rabbah ben Nahamani died, and at the moment of death, he uttered his answer, resolving the legal question.

In a kabbalistic text that appeared sometime in the fourteenth century, and hence later than the Zohar, it is told that Elijah brought the sage, Elkanah, to the Heavenly Academy where the angels became incensed at one "born of woman" in their midst. In this legend found in the introduction to *Sefer hapeli'ah*[8]—and likely based upon the zoharic story we are discussing—Elkanah became terrified and requested that Elijah bring him back to earth.

These various legends represent a number of different scenarios involving a sage from this world present in the Heavenly Academy or in the World-to-Come. Rabbi Joshua ben Levi was allowed to remain and hence to avoid experiencing death, whereas Rabbah bar Nahamani died when there was need for his knowledge in the Heavenly Academy. The zoharic writer recast the basic shared outline of these legends, choosing as his own option an order of expulsion.

Spanish literature of the thirteenth century includes a striking parallel to the sage's expulsion from the Heavenly Academy until his proper time of death. Based upon an older Latin account of St. Orea, Gonzola de Berceo's *Vida de Santa Oria* describes the saint's visionary ascent to heaven where, seeing her reward in the symbol of a throne, she is told that she must, nevertheless, return to earth and continue her ascetic life until her death. Lacking any choice, she accepts this message with pronounced sadness. Her vision, interestingly, includes a description of exceedingly luminous gems.[9]

The emphasis, within the description, given to winged heavenly beings populating the scene of the Heavenly Academy, has an archetypal ring which suggests a very different vantage point from which to read this story. The pattern of mystic flight, symbolized by wings and winged beings, and the access to the upper world and its celestial academy prior to physical death, recall a prevalent complex in primitive religion, one given most compact form in the other worldly journey of the shaman, dependent upon ecstatic trance.[10] Such a comparison does not suggest any direct contact with or influence of shamanism; however, the parallel might bring some of the contours of the story into sharper focus. The shaman was able to enter the realm of the departed or of celestial beings without actually shedding his physical form; through the impetus of his ecstatic trance, he was able to penetrate the bounds of earthly life without dying.

Placed against the image of that widespread religious complex, the story of Rabbi Hiyya emphatically denies the possibility of a mortal being allowed to transcend earthly bounds without first undergoing death. If the shaman's ecstatic trance enabled his journey, Rabbi Hiyya's expulsion signifies a bursting of that ecstasy which accompanied his visionary experience of ecstatic brightness. He is banished from ecstasy itself and exiled to an earthbound reality. This expulsion from ecstasy flows, we note in the narrative, from the realization of an unredeemed world, and, moreover, an unredeemed divinity as evident in the Exile of the Shekhinah. It is this encounter, even amid such effulgence, with the fact of an unredeemed world that removes the mystic from his visionary world.

The vision in the Zohar account serves to confirm the truth and the exulted worth of the teachings of bar Yohai. In this sense, it stands as a confirmation of the Zohar itself, which claims to include bar Yohai's teachings and revelations; the seal of approval that the Messiah and the angel (identified in commentaries as Metatron) place upon the teachings of bar Yohai constitutes a seal of approval for the

Zohar. In the Heavenly Academy of bar Yohai, the reader understands, it is Kabbalah that is studied, the same Kabbalah, though with
greater access to mystic truth, studied in this world.

If this be the case, then the experience of Rabbi Hiyya in the
higher worlds—including the experience of expulsion—holds true for
every devotee of the same mystic truth on this side of eternity. The
student of Kabbalah has caught a glimpse of the bliss of a higher
realm without having passed through the gateway of death. He has
wandered into a realm of awesome radiance beyond the sphere where
one can normally journey while still in a human state. Such a person
is as one who has intruded into an alien realm. And having caught a
glimpse of the higher world, he no longer fully belongs to this world.
The devotee is essentially, like Rabbi Hiyya at the end of the account,
a person suspended between two worlds and consequently alien to
both.

The motif of the Prince of the Sea in the story appears as a rem-
nant of much older traditions, prebiblical mythological accounts
telling of the sea in rebellion against God (or a god) at the time of
creation. According to such ancient myths it was necessary to van-
quish the sea monster, a manifestation of a deity representing chaos,
in order that the creating deity might proceed to create the world.
This mythic contest is known largely from the Babylonian creation
account, *Enuma Elish*.[11] Echoes of this kind of myth are found not
only in biblical poetry, where they serve as poetic embellishment and
imagery, but also in talmudic and midrashic sources.

In *Pirke derabbi eli'ezer*, chapter 5, it is related that following the
formation of dry land, the seas wish once again to regain their former
power and to cover the earth. According to *Shemot rabbah* 15:22,
God kills the sea (a monster and a force for chaos) along with those
waters that have rebelled. The zoharic passage under discussion
would seem to echo that basic motif found also in Baba Batra 74b
and *Bamidbar rabbah* 18:22; there God is reported as instructing the
sea to open its mouth and swallow all the waters of creation. When
the sea refuses, God kicks and kills the sea.

In the echo of this motif, found in the zoharic story we are discussing, the sea willingly agrees to God's request that it swallow the waters at the opportune moment. The crossing of the sea upon dry land signals the triumph of God as sole master of the seas and the ultimate triumph of order over chaos; it also symbolizes the redemption-to-come and the ingathering of the exiles (Isaiah 11:15). In a radical transformation, a thoroughly harmonistic rendition of the motif of the rebellion of the waters has completely negated the conflict central to that very motif.

Another echo of this same ancient motif is evident in a zoharic passage (2:113b) relating to the aftermath of the making of the Golden Calf and of Moses' shattering the Tablets of the Law. The ocean, we read there, responds by overflowing and flooding the entire world; the waters justify their behavior, maintaining that the world and its order exist by virtue of the Law, which had now been rejected. Moses, however, through a magical act, is able to prevent the waters from restoring the world to chaos; he takes water from the sea and pours it upon the site where he had burned the molten calf. Only this act appeases and quiets the waters.

Together, these two passages indicate that traces of the ancient tradition of opposition by the waters—one which in its earlier form predates the biblical period and reflects a radically different world view—are reflected in the lore of the Zohar. Together with the talmudic legends recalled by certain episodes of the narrative, the echo of ancient myth indicates the many layers of tradition reflected in this story of the aftermath of Bar Yohai's death.

Notes

1. *Devarim rabbah* 11:101; Baba Batra 17a.
2. Tamid 32b.
3. John Donne, "Holy Sonnet," in *The Complete Poetry of John Donne,* ed. John T. Shawcross, 342; Donne, "Elegie," in *The Poems of John Donne,* ed. Herbert Grierson, 442-443.
4. Baba Metsiah 85b.
5. Shabbat 88b-89a.
6. Ketubot 77b.

7. Baba Metsiah 86a.

8. See Louis Ginzberg, *Legends of the Jews*, 4:229-30; 6:337. The story is quoted in Michele Oron, *Hapeli'ah ve'hakaneh*, 339-40.

9. T. Anthony Perry, *Art and Meaning in Berceo's* Vida de Santa Oria, especially 39, 53-54, 110; John Esten Keller, *Pious Brief Narrative in Medieval Castilian and Galician Verse*; and Simina M. Farcasiu, "The Exegesis and Iconography of Vision in Gonzola de Berceo's *Vida de Santa Oria*," 305.

10. Mircea Eliade, *Myths, Rites, Symbols*, 1:233-43, 274; Eliade, *Myths, Dreams and Mysteries*, 102-5.

11. James B. Pritchard, *Ancient Near Eastern Texts*, 62-72.

The Sefirah of Ḥesed, Lovingkindness.

The Book of Adam: Two Accounts

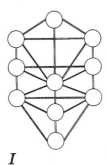

A book given to Adam in the Garden of Eden flew away when he was expelled, but with his pleading to God, it was restored to him.

I

Rabbi Abba said, "A book was actually given from above to the First Man, and through it he became acquainted with the higher Wisdom. That same book was then given to the 'sons of God,' the wise of the generation, and all who were privileged to study it learned the higher wisdom. That book was given to the First Man from the Master of Mysteries,[1] with three messengers[2] appointed to deliver it to him. When Adam was about to leave the Garden of Eden, he took that book with him, but when he actually left, it swiftly flew away. He prayed and cried before his Master, and the book was returned to him as before, so that this Wisdom would not be lost to humankind, and so that humans might endeavor to acquire knowledge of their Master. Similarly we have learned that Enoch had a book from the very same place from which the Book of the Generations of Adam had come . . ."(1:37b)

II

"This is the book of the generations of Adam"—of those in his likeness. Rabbi Isaac said, "The Holy One, blessed be He, showed to Adam the image of all those generations that would come to be in the world, together with all the sages of the world and the world's kings appointed to have political power over Israel. When his perception reached as far ahead as the time of David and he noted that David, king of Israel, died immediately upon his birth, Adam offered, "I'll give him seventy years of my own designated years." So seventy years were transferred from those originally assigned to Adam, and the Holy One, blessed be He, gave them instead to David. And concerning this David uttered words of praise, "'You have gladdened me by Your deeds, O Lord; I shout for joy at Your handiwork' (Psalms 92:5). What was the cause of my joy in the world? Your work— the First Man, who is actually of Your own making and not of the making of flesh and blood, as he alone came from the hands of God rather than being formed of humans, born of woman." In this way, seventy years were subtracted from the thousand years originally assigned to Adam.

The Holy One, blessed be He, went on to show him all the sages of all the generations until they came to the generation of Rabbi Akiva. Adam saw Akiva's torah and rejoiced; upon seeing his death, however, he was distressed. He then uttered the words, "How weighty Your thoughts seem to me, O God, how great their number" (Psalms 139:17).[3]

"This is the book" (Genesis 5:1)—Indeed there was a book, as it has been taught (1:37b) that when Adam was in the Garden of Eden, God sent down to him a book; it was given to him by Raziel,[4] the holy angel appointed over the mysteries of the holy worlds, and contained celestial engravings and holy wisdom, and seventy-two kinds of wisdom were explained by means of six hundred and seventy engravings of celestial mysteries. In the middle part of the book were engravings of wisdom to inform him of fifteen hundred keys that had not been disclosed even to the holy celestial beings; they were all concealed and sealed in this book until that time that it was given over to Adam.

The celestial angels gathered to hear that same wisdom and to acquire it, and they said, "Exult Yourself over the heavens, O God, let Your glory be over all the earth" (Psalms 57:12). Just then Hadarniel,[5] a holy angel, intimated to him, calling, "Adam, Adam, conceal the precious thing that has been given to you, for permission has not been granted to the celestial ones to know the greatness of

Your Master. You alone are so privileged." So Adam concealed the book and kept it with him until he left the Garden of Eden. In that earlier period, he studied it, occupying himself all that day[6] with the concealed knowledge of his Master, and he discovered the higher mysteries of which even the celestial servants are unaware.

When he sinned, transgressing his Master's command, the book flew away from him. Adam then beat his head and went into the water of the Gihon[7] up to his neck until his body become moldy and his brightness[8] vanished. At that moment, the Holy One, blessed be He, signaled to Raphael[9] to return that book to Adam, and he did so. Adam then continued to study it, and he gave it to his son, Seth, and similarly it reached all the following generations until it came into the hands of Abraham, who, through that book, knew to discern the greatness of the Master. And it is said that also to Enoch a book was given and he, too, grasped through it the glory of the Eternal One. (1:55ab)

Notes

1. Metatron or Raziel.

2. A talmudic passage (Baba Metsiah 86b), in referring to the three angels (messengers) who visited Abraham (Genesis 18), identifies the angels as Michael, Gabriel, and Raphael.

3. The previous verse, Psalms 139:16, reads, "Your eyes saw my unformed limbs; they were all recorded in Your book; in due time they were formed . . ." Rabbi Akiva, a second-century sage, met his death at the hands of the Romans, who had forbidden the teaching of Torah.

4. Raziel, the angel appointed over the higher secrets of God (*Raz*, "secret," *El*, "God"). Raziel is said to reveal the teachings of God and to disclose what has been decreed above; situated behind the veil that secludes the divine Throne, he has access to divine secrets and happenings. According to a midrashic tradition (*Pesikta rabbati*, chapter 20, piska 4, ed. Meir Friedmann, 96a-98b; also *Haggadat shema yisra'el*, in *Beit hamidrash*, ed. Adolf Jellinek, 5:164-65; and *Ma'ayan hakhmah*, in *Beit hamidrash*, ed. A. Jellinek, 1:601), the prophet Elijah, at Sinai, was able to hear what Raziel relayed from above and transmitted further that same knowledge (Louis Ginzberg, *Legends* 3:112). In some of these sources, Raziel is identified with the angel Gallitzur (*gle*, "disclose"; *tsur*, "rock").

5. Mentioned in *Pesikta rabbati*, chapter 20, as one of the angels whom Moses encountered when he ascended Mount Sinai to receive the Torah. There Hadarniel (*hadar*, "majesty") ceased to terrorize Moses, who had

entered the heavenly realm and instead became his guide along the dangerous route.

6. In a reading of the account of the First Man in rabbinic aggadah, Adam's creation, sin, and expulsion are considered to have all occurred within the span of a single day (*Vayikra rabbah*, chapter 6; Sanhedrin 38a and parallels).

7. The motif is found in *Pirke derabbi eli'ezer*, chapter 20.

8. The motif of Adam's initial iridescence that was lost with his sin is found in *Bereshit rabbah* 12:6.

9. The angel, commissioned with bringing healing to the earth (1:46b), later gave remedies and magical formulas to Noah (*Sefer no'ah*, note commentary that follows).

Commentary

Unlike the other stories included in this collection, neither of the above passages constitutes an extended, developed narrative. While these passages in themselves do not stand out like the others as significant examples of narrative art, they do, nevertheless, provide an extremely interesting case study of the retelling of a much older tradition. These passages remold an older motif to express an underlying ambiguity within the world view of the Zohar.

Because the particular motif found in the above two passages certainly predates the Zohar, a comprehensive examination of the zoharic passages requires an examination of the prior history of the motif.

A biblical verse, *ze sefer toledot adam* (This is the record of Adam's line) Genesis 5:1, serves as proof text of the motif. While the word *sefer* came to be understood as "book," the words of this verse, it is generally maintained, do not indicate anything like an actual book. The understanding of the word *sefer* as "book" dates back only to postbiblical times, while the biblical use of the same word indicates rather a written document or record.[1] Cassutto[2] explains the word as based on the Akkadian root meaning "to send," maintaining that the word *sefer* originally indicated a written document sent from one place to another, and later came to refer to anything written. Cassutto explains the use of the word in Genesis 5:1, by positing that the genealogical list introduced by the verse is not the type of thing that would have been recited orally and hence is referred to as *sefer*, something normally recorded in writing.[3]

Among medieval commentators, both Rashi and Kimchi understood the word sefer in that verse not as a book but as relating rather to the root *spr*, "counting," a counting of the generations beginning with Adam. Sforno understood the word as related to the same root, *spr*, in the sense of "telling," in this case recounting the happenings of the human race.

A talmudic source found in Avodah Zarah 5a explains the verse as follows: God shows all the generations to the First Man, each generation with its interpreters of the Torah, its sages, and those having financial responsibility for the affairs of the community. This source mentions that Adam saw Rabbi Akiva among the sages; he rejoiced in Akiva's learning but was distressed at the latter's martyred death, the very legend retold in the second of our zoharic passages above.[4] According to a tradition preserved in other sources, such as *Midrash tehillim* 92:10, *Bamidbar rabbah* 14:12, *Pirke derabbi eli'ezer*, chapter 19, and *Yalkut shimoni* 1:41, Adam discovered that no life span whatsoever had been granted to David, and he volunteered to reduce his own thousand-year life by seventy years, which were then given to David. This legend, too, is included in the second of our zoharic passages on the subject of the book of Adam.

The same verse is explained in another rabbinic source, *Avot derabbi natan*,[5] as God showing Adam all the future generations as though they were then in existence and living their lives in his presence. Elsewhere (*Bereshit rabbah* 24:2; note also *Avot derabbi natan*, second version, chapter 8) the same idea connects with a reading of Psalm 139. There, in the name of Rabbi Judah bar Simeon, it is related that while the First Man still lay formless in the presence of his Maker, God showed to him each generation with its interpreters of the Torah, its sages, scribes, and leaders. A biblical proof text is provided—"Your eyes saw my unformed limbs; they were all recorded in Your book" (Psalms 139:16)—and it is added, "The unformed state Your eyes beheld is written upon the Book of the First Man. 'This is the book (*sefer*) of the generations of Adam'" (Genesis 5:1). In this passage, the word *sefer* is clearly understood as a book. A further comment is found in *Bereshit rabbah* 24:4: "The messianic king will not come until all those souls that God intended (which rose in God's thought) are actually created. And these are the souls written in the Book of the First Man" (found also in *Vayikra rabbah* 15:1).

Another talmudic source, Baba Metsiah 86a, states that when Rabbi Judah the Prince was unable by force of circumstances to ordain Samuel, the physician who had healed him, the former told him that he had seen the Book of Adam and that there it was written that the physician will be referred to as a *ḥakham* (sage) but will not be ordained and called "rabbi." In his comment upon this passage, Rashi explained the Book as that which God showed Adam and which contained all the generations and their sages.[6]

Interpreting the same verse from Psalms 139, a source recorded in *Midrash tehillim* 139:6 speaks of God's having written in His book all that He will bring about through Adam (and his posterity) until the time of resurrection at the end of days. *Midrash tanḥuma* (ed. Solomon Buber, Bereshit 28), referring to the same verse from Psalms 139, states that God showed to the First Man all the generations up to the Resurrection and adds that all that Adam saw is written in his book; included, it is specified, are the precise dates of the exodus from Egypt, the crossing of the Reed Sea, and the giving of the Torah.

Some passages in the classical sources stress a more abstract nature of the book of Adam, while others seem to suggest an actual book containing knowledge of the future generations of the human race. A passage in *Shemot rabbah* 40:2, for example, relates that upon receiving the command to construct the artifacts of the Tabernacle, Moses did not know who was actually to construct them.

(God) said to him, "I will show you." And what did the Holy One do? He brought to him the book of Adam and showed him all the generations destined to appear from the Creation until the Resurrection of the Dead, each generation and its kings, leaders and prophets. He said to him, "Each one I designated already from that very hour, and similarly I designated Bezalel at that time." And so, "I have called upon the name Bezalel." (Exodus 31:2)

The motif of the disclosure of the book telling of the future generations appears in connection with Moses also in *Vayikra rabbah*
26:17 and in *Eliyahu zuta*, chapter 6.

Louis Ginzberg[7] explained this concept of a Book of Adam as the
Jewish form of a view, prevalent among the Babylonians, that the
totality of divine knowledge and of destiny is written on tablets containing even the names of kings who will rule along with the destiny
of individuals. The ancient Babylonian creation epic, *Enuma elish*,
relates that the Babylonian high god, Marduk, took the "Tablets of
Fate (or Destinies)" from Kingu, his adversary, and then proceeded
to seal them.[8] This conception, A. Jeremias pointed out,[9] is echoed in
various biblical sources: for example, in Exodus 32:32, where Moses
requested that God erase Moses' name from His book if He will not
forgive Israel.[10] The same concept is present also in Jubilees 30:20,
which speaks of Levi's name having been recorded on the "heavenly
tablets," and in numerous passages in the Books of Enoch.[11] In the
latter, Enoch is shown the heavenly tablets and is told to read from
those holy books that record the deeds of mankind through the
course of all the generations extending to that time when sin will
vanish from the world. In ancient Mesopotamia this same conception
was connected with the annual rites when, it was believed, the destiny
of every person was recorded and sealed, a conception and even a
phraseology that has survived in the Jewish liturgy of the High Holy
Days.[12]

A grasp of this ancient Near Eastern idea leads one to understand
the phrase *sefer toledot adam* as just such a heavenly book containing
the history of the human race, a knowledge of future generations
given to Adam at the very onset of human history. The particular
thrust of this concept is mirrored also in significantly later expressions
of the motif of the book of Adam.

Gershom Scholem,[13] in discussing the motif of God's having
shown all the generations to Adam, has focused upon the detail that
this revelation occurred while Adam was in an amorphous, unformed
state (golem) prior to his receiving a soul and the capacities of speech
and thought. According to Scholem, the motif conveys that in that
unformed state, a power emanating from the earth itself, the source
of his body, enabled the First Man to experience a vision encompassing all the generations.

Whereas in earlier, classical sources, the tradition of the book of Adam is preserved in very brief statements, the motif is expanded into a longer narrative in a medieval text, the second recension of *Sefer no'aḥ*.[14] There we read that following his sin and expulsion from Eden, Adam was worried that his wisdom had been taken from him, in particular his knowledge of future happenings. He prayed, begging for precise knowledge of what would occur to him and to his descendents. His pleading was answered when the angel Raziel appeared with a book; the angel told him that with this book he would know what would happen to him until the time of his death. Furthermore, the angel told him, if his children and descendents followed basic instructions concerning the spirit in which the book was to be read, they too would have knowledge of the future including such matters as weather, plagues, abundance, and hunger. Enoch, it is told, later concealed the book, and so before the Flood, the angel Raphael appeared to Noah to give him that same book. With it Noah was able to learn of future happenings and to understand how he might escape from destruction in the waters of the Flood and how to build the ark.[15] There is reason to believe that the tradition found in *Sefer no'aḥ* is related to the lore of Ashkenazic pietism, which, in turn, drew upon still earlier traditions going back to the talmudic period.

The nature of the book of Adam, as discussed in *Sefer no'aḥ*, mirrors the Babylonian conception that human destiny is written out, in detail, in a celestial book. That more abstract concept, however, quite clearly merges with the sense of a concrete book.

The Zohar includes a number of "quotations" brought in the name of the Book of Adam. Some of these quotations relate what is to occur at a future time. "On that day that the Temple will be completed, the Fathers will awaken song in both the upper and the lower worlds" (2:143b). Another such "quotation" foretells the coming of Elijah, described as a spirit clothed in a physical body but also able to exchange that body for a luminous one, thus allowing him to exist "as an angel among angels," yet always able to retrieve his material body again (2:197a). Elsewhere, it is reported that "a *ḥaver* ['fellow,' a student of mystic wisdom] living in the South had seen in the books of the ancients and in the Book of Adam" certain information such as the number of earths and firmaments, the spherelike shape of the inhabited world, bizarre races of people resulting from various atmospheric differences, day occurring where elsewhere it is night, and a place where there is virtually only day, and the like (3:9b-10a). In addition, the Book of Adam is mentioned as a source for knowledge of metoposcopy, the reading of a person's character as it is revealed through his facial features (2:70b).

Just as in earlier sources, some passages in the Zohar convey the concept of *sefer toledot adam* in a thoroughly abstract way, independent of any reference to an actual or concrete book. Posing as a rhetorical question, "And did he [Adam] have a book?", one such passage explains:

This is not taken to mean simply that (Adam) saw by means of the capacity of prophecy that these future generations were destined to appear in the world, as one foreseeing the future, but rather that he actually saw—with his own eyes—the form in which they would exist in the world. This was possible because from the day of the world's creation, all those souls destined to live as human beings were present before God in the form that they would later assume on earth. (1:90b; see also 1:227b)

In contrast, we have already noted in the first of our two zoharic passages on this motif (1:37b) that "God did indeed send down a book to Adam by means of which he came to know the higher wisdom" (1:37b). In the second passage (1:55a-b), both tendencies are present: God showed to Adam the images of all the generations destined to appear and their significant representatives including David and Akiva, and God also sent the angel Raziel to give Adam a book—an actual book.

These zoharic legends would appear to be further developments of the kind of legend of the book of Adam found in that second recension of the Book of Noah.[16] But if the zoharic legends on this motif were influenced by *Sefer no'ah* or by a source similar to it, those same zoharic passages suggest that their author also altered the earlier form of the legend in subtle but significant ways.

The character of the Book of Adam is described in *Sefer no'ah* essentially as a disclosure of the future course of history along with certain practical instructions. In the zoharic accounts that same Book of Adam is said to contain mysteries of the higher world. This definition of the content of the book of Adam would appear to allude to the very subject and content of the Zohar itself. It is through the book of Adam that the latter came to know *ḥokhmata ila'ah* (the higher wisdom), and like the book of Enoch, which is said to have come from the same source, it contains the *raza diḥokhmata* (the mysteries of wisdom 1:37b). In our second zoharic passage (1:55b), the book is described as containing *ḥokhmah kadisha* (holy wisdom). In other words, the book of Adam, as grasped in the zoharic legend, is understood as a virtual mirror of the Zohar itself consisting of mysteries of the higher realms. The author of the Zohar was understandably attracted to the motif of the giving of a book of wisdom to the human race at the onset of human history, a wisdom in effect identified with its own teaching. More precisely, in the motif of the book of Adam, the Zohar found an image through which to speak of itself and its own kind of wisdom. The Zohar utilized these older legends as a language in which to express its understanding of itself.

While according to *Sefer no'aḥ*, the book is given to Adam after his expulsion from Eden and the subsequent loss of his prior wisdom, in this zoharic legend the book flies away at the time of the expulsion from Eden. Its absence, it would appear, partakes of the very nature of exile itself, of the larger "human condition" beginning with the expulsion from Paradise. Yet upon Adam's pleading, the book is restored to him. This form of the legend might imply that with Kabbalah one aspect of the very nature of exile is, in fact, nullified; what follows is an exile qualified spiritually by our possession of mystic wisdom—to whatever degree man can be said to possess it. The book is returned to Adam both because of the latter's supplication and weeping and because God has concurred that it is important that the book with its higher wisdom remain in human hands.

The zoharic retelling of the legend conveys a strong note of ambivalence, as God wills and yet does not will that man should acquire the secret knowledge. This ambivalence of divine intent brings to mind a similar ambivalence on the part of bar Yohai himself in the *Idra rabba* (3:127b) as to whether he should disclose the deepest secrets and mystic teachings. Bar Yohai realizes the danger of revealing those mysteries of the very highest wisdom to his students, and yet he feels obligated to reveal them for the reason that the world is in need of them.

The Zohar's retelling of the older tradition adds at least one significant element to the basic story: the loss of the book after it has initially been given. The motif of the mysterious loss of a book—or of knowledge or memory or wisdom—is present also in other narrative passages within the Zohar text, and we cannot read this particular element of the zoharic legend of the book of Adam in isolation from those passages.

In another zoharic story which relates to the book of Adam (1:117b-118a), Rabbi Yose, during the course of a journey, recalls that long ago at the very site they had reached, his father had told him that at the age of sixty, he would find a treasure of sublime wisdom. Moreover, his father had told him that upon finding the treasure, fire would touch his hands and he would lose that wisdom he had discovered. It then happens that in a cave, Rabbi Yose discovers a book placed in a cleft of the rock wall, a book containing seventy-two engravings of letters that had been given to Adam. Through these engravings Adam knew "all the wisdom concerning the highest holy beings and those impure shells situated behind the mill [an intermediary sefirah] which turns beyond the veil among the unseen celestial essences. And through them he knew all that was destined to occur in the world until that day that a cloud will arise from the West to cast the world into utter darkness."

When Rabbi Yose, together with Rabbi Yehuda, begins to study the book, to grasp its mysteries and to discuss them, "a flame of fire, impelled by a strong gust of wind, appeared and struck their hands. And the book vanished from their sight." Perplexed, the two sages come to Rabbi Simeon bar Yohai who inquires whether they had been reading in these engravings concerning the time of the Messiah's coming. They cannot answer, for when the book vanished from their sight, they completely forgot all that they had read in the book. Their forgetting unambiguously confirms the divine will evident in the book's disappearance and makes for a double-disappearance—even though the manuscript had come to Rabbi Yose as a fulfillment of his father's paradoxical prophecy.

In the narrative passage, Rabbi Simeon informs the two sages that it is not God's will "that so much be revealed to the world," but explains that in the future, approaching the time of the Messiah's coming, even young children will be able to discover "the secrets of wisdom and through them will know the times and calculations of Redemption."

While the direct thrust of this story relates to messianic calculations (and the story in this respect echoes a talmudic legend concerning Jonathan ben Uzziel [Megillah 3a]), this story shares the same surrealistic motif of a loss of writings with other narrative passages in the Zohar, passages unrelated to the subject of messianic calculations. In one such story (2:13a-b), a stranger, upon wandering into a marvelous cave, is handed a bundle of writings. But when he later presents the writings to Rabbi Eleazar and the latter opens the bundle, a ray of fire appears all around him, and before he can look at them, the writings fly away from his hands.

In still another account (1:216b-217a), telling of the aftermath of the death of Rabbi Simeon bar Yohai, Rabbi Yehuda, in a dream, sees Rabbi Simeon ascending upon four wings together with a Torah scroll and all the books of higher mysteries and lore, bringing them up with him to the heavens until they all disappear from view. It is stated there that only a small measure, one *omer*, of that wisdom remains, presumably the Zohar itself, surviving the loss of an infinite reservoir of higher wisdom in the person of Rabbi Simeon.

These various stories convey the ephemeral nature of the higher wisdom, which is never truly or permanently within our grasp. This realization adds to the preciousness of that higher wisdom a human being is able to possess—even if it be but an *omer* of the mystic knowledge of bar Yohai. Furthermore, as suggested in some of these stories, mystic wisdom vanishes when it becomes the subject of human communication.[17] When Rabbi Yose begins discussing the contents of the engravings with Rabbi Yehuda, the book vanishes through fire, and when the stranger hands the documents in his trust to another person who opens them, they immediately fly away. True, the motif of the Book of Adam, as retold in the Zohar, becomes a symbol of messianic calculations in the Zohar, but in a larger sense it serves also as a vehicle of the Zohar's own self-perception, a deepened marvel of the glimpse of mystic truth which, even considering its basically ephemeral nature, remains in human possession.

This theme of disappearance is found in various passages in the pages preceding the legends of the book of Adam in the Zohar's exegesis on Bereshit. Rabbi Hamnuna, it is related (1:7a), comes from the "other world" to reveal mysteries to the Fellows, but before they are able to recognize him, he disappears. A few pages later, the reader notes the comment that the human being lacks the permanence that marks the higher, angelic beings, a thematic note that relates also to the Creator's efforts to give a quality of permanence to the world (1:19b). The light created on the first day was given and then withdrawn (1:31b-32a), to be restored only at a future time of messianic fulfillment.

In the first of the zoharic passages translated above (1:37b), no angels' names are mentioned; in the second (1:55a-b), it is Raziel who initially gives the book to Adam, though following the latter's sin and expulsion from Eden, the angel Raphael is ordered to return the book. In a highly illuminating study of the zoharic interpretation of the change that came over the world with Adam's sin, D. Cohen-Aloro[18] has emphasized this detail in terms of the general role and connotations of Raphael as an angel connected with healing and remedies and, by association, also with magic. In her study, she concludes that the book given to Adam the second time—by Raphael—is of a decidedly lower character; it reflects the new reality that came into being with Adam's sin, a world dominated by Satan and one to which man could relate by means of magic. In her reading of the motif of the book of Adam in the Zohar, the book restored to Adam with his expulsion from Eden has a markedly negative significance and stands in contrast with the original book given to him. While the second book contains all kinds and levels of wisdom, it is essentially a wisdom oriented to the material world and the means to control it and to finding protection from evil forces given free rein in the fallen world.

Cohen-Aloro examines the subject of *Sefer adam* in the Zohar as a representation of a world man can relate to through magic. This same subject, however, bears other nuances that point in very different directions. Though the book of Adam does acquire negative significance as a book capable of leading man astray from God, it also has a most positive significance in that through that book Abraham came to the true faith (1:55b), and also through his reading of the

book, Noah arrived at an understanding of the correct forms of
divine service (1:58b).

The import of *Sefer adam* in the Zohar has to be examined also
in terms of the particular explanation of idolatry and pagan worship,
which, we will suggest, is expressed precisely by means of the complex role of the book of Adam. In this, too, the motif of the book of
Adam serves as a vehicle of the Zohar's self-perception as it voices a
basic ambiguity that cuts across the text.

In *Sefer no'ah*, we read that when Adam is expelled from Eden
and receives the book from the angel Raziel, the angel counsels him
on the spirit in which to study this book: namely, with purity, humility, and obedience.

Implicit in this precaution is the possibility that the book might
be studied in an improper spirit. The negative implication of this
warning, which, according to *Sefer no'ah*, accompanied the giving of
the book, echoes in various passages in the Zohar. True, we are
informed that Noah "studied the Book of Adam and also the Book of
Enoch with diligence . . . and learned from them the appropriate
forms by which to worship God" (the sacrifices, 1:58b). The counter-
possibility, however, generally proves to be the case. We read that
whenever God "allowed the deep mysteries of that wisdom to
descend to the world, they served to corrupt mankind, who, in their
wake, attempted to provoke God. To Adam God gave the higher wisdom, but the First Man utilized that disclosed wisdom to become
familiar also with the lower grades until, ultimately, he attached himself to the evil inclination" (1:75b-76a). While not mentioning a
Book of Adam, this passage speaks in terms of the more general concept of higher wisdom having been revealed to Adam. The reader is
told that the same occurred also with the generations following
Adam; they used the same primordial books and knowledge to rebel
against God, as did various peoples among whom fragments of that
ancient wisdom had been disseminated. "Rabbi Simeon said, 'Had I
been alive when the Holy One, blessed be He, gave the books of
Enoch and Adam to humankind, I would have endeavored to with-
hold their dissemination because not all people read them with the

correct intent; instead they derived from them distorted ideas which lead men away from the service of the Most Exulted One to the worship of strange powers'" (1:72b). Another zoharic passage speaks of the Wisdom of the *b'ne kedem* ("the children of the East," 1:100a, 133b) received through the patriarch Abraham when he transmitted it to his other children while reserving the purest wisdom for Isaac. "Rabbi Abba said, 'I once chanced to be in a town where the descendents of the 'children of the East' lived, and they taught me some of the ancient wisdom with which they were familiar. They also had in their possession books containing their wisdom.'" While Rabbi Abba noted in their books passages completely in consonance with the particular idea presented in the Zohar text at that point, he also noted in the same books rites and ceremonies connected with the worship of the stars. The books contained the proper directions for concentrating one's thoughts upon the heavenly bodies so as to draw (their spirits) nearer the worshipper. Rabbi Abba then explained to his own children that while he had found in those books teachings

which are similar to what we learn in our own Torah, it is nevertheless necessary to keep distant from these books so that your hearts might not be influenced to perform the pagan services and seek the powers to which the books refer. Be careful not to come under their influence and to depart, God forbid, from the worship of the Holy One, since all these books mislead people. For the ancient children of the East possessed a wisdom they had received from Abraham who transmitted it to the sons of the concubines. . . . In the course of time, they followed the way of that wisdom into many distressful directions. (1:99b-100a)

A still more pronounced ambiguity concerning idolatrous practices is evident in the following zoharic story:

Once Rabbi Yose and Rabbi Hiyya were walking together, continuing on their way until darkness fell. Then they sat down and discussed various subjects until dawn when they continued on their way. Rabbi Hiyya commented, "Look at dawn breaking through in the eastern sky. At this moment all the children of the East who live among the mountains of light will be worshipping that light which announces

the imminent appearance of the sun. The sun itself has many worshippers, but these are the worshippers of its messenger which they
call "the god of the shining pearl," and their oath is "Allah of the
shining pearl." Yet, do not suppose that this worship is false and
empty of substance; rather, it actually contains a wisdom known from
the earliest days. Before sunrise, when the light of dawn is first seen,
an angel appointed to direct the sun appears with the holy letters of
the heavenly blessed Name inscribed upon his brow; with the power
of those letters he first opens all the windows of the heavens and then
flies away. Then he enters within the aura of brightness surrounding
the sun and waits there until the sun rises to cast its light over all the
world. And that very angel, the sun's guardian, is appointed also over
gold and rubies. It if for this reason that sun-worshippers and the
devotees of the dawn worship that angel, for through various spots
and signs which they have received from earlier tradition and which
they also detect in the sun they are able to identify the place of gold
and rubies. (2:188a)

This narrative passage conveys both an appreciation and a con-
demnation of pagan worship. (Although the name Allah is mentioned, the sense of the worship is decidedly pagan; the Zohar, in
fact, viewed both Christianity and Islam very much as pagan religions.) Such worship, it is conveyed, is not empty of substance but is
rather a misinterpretation or misunderstanding both of the splendor
of nature and of an ancient wisdom going back to much earlier days.

The reader notes a similar pattern within the zoharic exegesis that
traces the magic arts and the divination of Bilaam to the Fallen
Angels, Aza and Aza'el (3:208a). In this detail, the Zohar locates the
source of magical knowledge and practices in those who are both
angels and in a fallen state. Those arts and their wisdom are hence of
celestial origin even while they are transformed by a state of fallen-
ness. The magic arts are never negated or denied; they are considered
to be true, but at the same time, like idolatry, they comprise a partial
truth severed from their larger, more complete context, and as such
they are more likely than not to be misused. Their source lay in real
forces in the upper worlds and they are therefore efficacious even
though that source is not located in the very highest powers (2:52b).

The theurgic nature of a considerable part of zoharic teaching and its practices—with its intent to influence the upper worlds and, indirectly, our world as well—might account for the Zohar's own ambivalent attitude toward magic, which is accepted as true even though its practice is forbidden. The same ambivalent attitude toward magical arts is evident in the zoharic traditions ascribing those arts to Adam. It is written that he took them from the Garden of Eden in the form of "knowledge of the leaves of the Tree," while it is claimed, at the same time, that neither he nor his family actually practiced such magic arts, which were later employed for purposes of evil and rebellion against God (1:56a).

Idolatry, to the mind of the Zohar's author, is a partial truth, rooted in the reality of the impure powers within the total cosmic scene. We read, for example, of "the celestial impure power which presided over the idolatrous act performed by Jeroboam and which was indispensable to his success" (2:67a). The zoharic author explains idolatry by referring to the actual existence of the Impure Spirit, who must be appeased in order to be subjugated (2:237b). Furthermore, the "gods" of the nations, mentioned in the Bible, we are told, are not mere idols but actual celestial figures with real (though limited) power in this world (2:7a).

These fragmentary narrative passages and comments from the Zohar all point to the idea that primordial knowledge, which is in itself celestial and holy—the kind of knowledge which the zoharic author believes can be identified with his own teachings—can be corrupted and placed in the service of the forces representing the antithesis of holiness. Or stated conversely: that which appears as pagan in nature, belief, and practice has its roots in what was disclosed by celestial powers or even by God Himself. While the two kinds of wisdom are not to be identified with one another, there is nevertheless a definite kinship between the two. For the zoharic author, both are rooted in the same theosophical reality.

It follows that the zoharic author, identifying his own teachings with the mysteries of the Book of Adam properly understood, conceived of the emergence of polytheism as a partial, and hence distorted, grasp of that same primordial wisdom ascribed to a divine source. The basis of the belief and worship of strange gods and of idolatrous practices including magic arts is precisely the reality of the *Sitra aḥra*, the impure powers countering the forces of holiness in the zoharic cosmic picture. Paganism, it follows, is not empty of substance, but contains a true, ancient wisdom in a partial and distorted state. In his *Book of the Pomegranate*,[19] Moses de Leon explains the origins of pagan worship simply as an innocent error of judgment, reflecting the opinion that the One God who created the universe wished humans to honor and worship the luminaries and stars; only during the course of time was the initial monotheistic belief lost, with the rites directed to the sun and stars taking on independent significance in an emerging polytheism. In this view, Moses de Leon was influenced by Maimonides,[20] an influence evident even in the particular wording of the statement. In contrast, numerous zoharic passages present a much more radical explanation of paganism: the zoharic author understands pagan religion—from its beginning—as the actual belief in other powers, a belief which—on one level—is not without validity. To the mind of the zoharic author, both its own true wisdom and paganism are derived from accurate and distorted readings, respectively, of the book of Adam and of similar primordial revelations.

In our own century, Gershom Scholem has forcefully spelled out his thesis that in the zoharic Kabbalah and its tradition, myth carved a place for itself within the very framework of a monotheistic faith, which, in its classical form, is largely the antithesis of myth.[21] Cosmic conflict, sacred marriage, and an unbounded imagination clothing itself in mythological imagery were all granted entrance into the world of Jewish belief. In its adaptation of the motif of the book of Adam and in parallel motifs, the mystic-author—in whose work we note such an abundance of archetypal images and concepts rooted in cross-cultural mythic patterns—might be disclosing something quite significant: his own concealed yet intuitive sense of the basic affinity of the zoharic teaching with that larger world of religious and mythic imagination and ritual which lies beyond the boundaries of what can be accommodated to Jewish monotheism. The zoharic author expresses a sense of the ultimate kinship of his teaching with something, at the same time, with which he clearly could not identify. The book of Adam, a motif with a long history, becomes—it would appear—a means by which the zoharic author voices that striking ambiguity.

Notes

1. Harry Orlinsky, *Notes on the New Translation of the Torah*, 71.
2. Umberto Cassutto, *Me'adam ve'ad no'ah*, 186.
3. Gerhard Von Rad (*Genesis*, 70) suggests that the text in Genesis 5:1 retains the title of an actual book of genealogy and the like, while Benno Jacob (*The First Book of the Bible—Genesis*, 41) states that the word *sefer* itself might refer also to shorter documents as would be the case in this verse.
4. The text of this talmudic passage denies there having been an actual book. Menahem Kasher (*Torah shelemah* 2:346) however, questions whether that denial, in the form of a statement, appears in earlier versions of the text.
5. Version A, chapter 31.
6. Solomon Funk, in *Monumenta Talmudica* I, 324, bringing Babylonian parallels which refer to the stars as the "writing of Heaven," understands Rabbi's statement as "I have seen it inscribed in the stars." This might be born out more readily if the statement were ascribed to Samuel, the physician, who elsewhere was referred to as Shmuel *yarhina'ah*, from *yare'ah*, "moon," because of his astronomical knowledge (Rosh Hashanah 20b).
7. Ginzberg, *Legends* 5:82, citing A. Jeremias, *Babylonisches im Neue Testament*, 69. Geo. Widengren, in his monograph, *The Ascension of the Apostle and the Heavenly Book*, explored the ancient Mesopotamian concept of the Heavenly Tablets or Book and its transmission to the king upon his enthronement, which occurred at the time of his ascension to the upper world. Widengren traced this concept through Hebrew and Gnostic traditions extending into the Islamic world.
8. James B. Pritchard, *Ancient Near Eastern Texts*, 93.
9. Jeremias, 69.
10. Note also Isaiah 4:3, Psalms 69:29 and Daniel 12:1-2 for the related concept of a book of life as well as such Christian texts as Luke 10:20, Philippians 4:3, Hebrews 12:23, and Revelations 3:5, 13:8, and 17:8, which speak of those names written in the Book of Life even before the very foundation of the world came into being.
11. Note in particular Enoch 47:3, 81:1-2, 93:2, 103:2, 106:19, 107:1, and 108:3 and 7.
12. E. A. Speiser, "Census and Ritual Expiation in Mari and Israel," 24; *At the Dawn of Civilization: The World History of the Jewish People*, ed. E. A. Speiser, 235.
13. Gershom Scholem, *On the Kabbalah and Its Symbolism*, 161-62.
14. Included in *Beit hamidrash* (ed. Adolph Jellinek), III, 156-59.
15. Parts of the text of that second recension of *Sefer no'ah* are found also in the Introduction to *Sefer razi'el*, which first appeared in Amsterdam in 1701 but which contains much earlier material.
16. Ginzberg, *Legends* 5:177, n. 23.
17. Note Gershom Scholem's "Ten Non-historical Articles on the

Kabbalah" as discussed in Joseph Dan, "*Min hasemel el hamesumal,*" 363-67, on the paradox inherent in the transmission of what is essentially incapable of transmission and communication in Kabbalah. 18. D. Cohen-Aloro, "The Zohar's View of Magic as a Consequence of the Original Sin."

19. Moses de Leon. *Book of the Pomegranate,* ed. Elliot Wolfson, 268.

20. Mishnah torah, *Hilkhot avodat kokhavim,* chap. 1.

21. Scholem, *On the Kabbalah and Its Symbolism,* 88-100; *Major Trends in Jewish Mysticism,* 34-35.

The Sefirah of Din, Judgment, also
Gevurah, Strength.

The House of the World

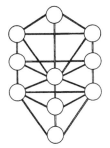

The basic structure of existence is constructed, threatened, and will ultimately be perfected as the defiling, threatening force is utterly removed.

"But Jacob journeyed on to Succoth, and built a house for himself and made stalls for his cattle; that is why the place was called Succoth" (Genesis 33:17).

Beginning his interpretation of this verse, Rabbi Hiyya referred to another verse: "Unless the Lord build the house, its builders labor in vain; unless the Lord watches over the city, the watchman keeps vigil in vain" (Psalms 127:1). He commented, "Come and note: At the moment that the first stirring to create a universe arose in the divine will, He brought forth from the spark of darkness[1] a mist which then glowed in the midst of the darkness. The light remained above even as it descended below, glistening in a hundred different paths—some hardly detectable and others expansive—bringing the House of the World into being.

"This House is situated at the very center of all that is. How many entrances and chambers it has! It is surrounded everywhere by concealed, holy places where the birds of the heavens build nests, each according to its own kind. From its midst there emerges a single large and mighty Tree, with thick branches and fruit, having abundant sustenance in it for all. That Tree ascends upward to the very clouds of the heavens, until it disappears from view among three mountains, and then comes into view both climbing higher and also descending. The House, nourished and watered by the Tree, conceals numerous celestial and unknown treasures. In this way that House was constructed and beautified. The Tree is visible during the daylight hours but at night is hidden from view, while the House, in contrast, is seen at night and is hidden from view during the day.

"At the hour that darkness sets in, the House appears, its door-ways all firmly closed in all directions. At once numerous spirits fly about in the air, seeking to enter and ascend within it, curious as to what it contains. They join with the birds, acquiring their knowledge and flying about and observing, until the darkness, now attached to the House, is awakened and sends forth a single flame and strikes with mighty hammers, opening the doors and cleaving the rocks. That flame then flares both up and down, striking the world, and voices are awakened both above and below.

"After connecting with air emerging from amidst the pillar of clouds of the inner altar and spreading out in all four directions, a herald immediately ascends and calls out. A million hosts stand to the left and a myriad of myriads[2] to the right, while the herald stands in his place, calling out forcefully. Then, so many there are who chant and worship! Two doors open, one to the south, the other to the north. The House ascends and stands, linking the two sides as song is chanted and words of praise ascend. Whoever then enters does so as in a whisper, and the House glistens with six exceedingly bright lights, illumining all directions. Streams of balsam flowing from there, watering all the wild beasts and the birds, as it is written, '[You make springs gust forth in torrents; they make their way between the hills] giving drink to all the wild beasts; the wild asses slake their thirst. The birds of the sky dwell beside them and sing among the foliage' (Psalms 104:10-12), and song continues until daybreak.

"Then when dawn appears, the stars and the constellations of the heavens and all their hosts chant songs of praise, as is written, '[Who set its cornerstone] when the morning stars sang together and all the divine beings shouted for joy?' (Job 38:6-7). And note, 'Unless the Lord builds the house, its builders labor in vain; unless the Lord watches over the city, the watchman keeps vigil in vain' (Psalms 127:1). This refers to the sublime King who is constantly engaged in constructing and perfecting that House. When? Whenever proper terrestrial worship and devotions ascend from below.

" 'Unless the Lord watches over the city [the watchman keeps vigil in vain]' (Psalms 127:1). To what time does this refer? To the hour that the darkness of evening sets in, when armed camps wander about through the world; the doors are closed and guarded from all sides to prevent any uncircumcised and unclean one from approaching, as it is stated, '[Awake, awake, O Zion! Clothe yourself in splendor; Put on your robes of majesty, Jerusalem, holy city!] For the uncircumcised and the unclean shall never enter you again' (Isaiah 52:1)—those whom, in the future, the Holy One, blessed be He, will remove from the world! Who, then, is the uncircumcised and who is the unclean one [to whom the verse refers]? Actually, they are one and the same, the very one who enticed [Adam and Eve] and whom they followed to cause death for all[3] and who continues to defile this House until that time when the Holy One, blessed be He, will expel him from the world."

And so it is, that "unless the Lord watches over the city, the watchman keeps vigil in vain" (Psalms 127:1).

(1:172ab)

Notes

1. Or Lamp of Darkness. On this term, see Moses De Leon, *Book of the Pomegranate*, ed. Elliot Wolfson, 81, no. 29; Daniel Matt, *Zohar*, 207-8, 297; and Yehuda Leibes, *Perakim bemillon sefer hazohar*, 146-51; 161-64; 327-31. In an ultimate sense, only this Supernal Spark exists; the existence of everything below it, including the *Sefirot*, is dependent upon this Spark.

2. One million.

3. Based on the identification of Satan with both the evil inclination and the Angel of Death; Baba Batra 16a.

Commentary

The hours of dawn and dusk, the alternation and marvel of light and darkness, was a source of fascination in Zoharic literature. The hour of dawn is painted in word images: "The person rising early to set out on a journey is told to look up, at a certain moment, to the eastern sky where, at daybreak, he will see something resembling letters appearing in movement, formed by sparks of the very letters of the alphabet with which God created the world".(2:130b, *Idra deve mashkena*).

That same fascination is also evident in our passage, a descriptive account that extends between the foci of dawn and of darkness.

Light and darkness, however, serve as a symbolic language in the hands of the zoharic author, who reveals his highly poetic tendencies in this passage. In the light of some basic kabbalistic symbols, this account can be understood as one that relates, with intricate allusion, the story of the formation of the world of the *Sefirot* including the Shekhinah, the conflict that threatens to endanger the Shekhinah, and the resolution of that conflict by the removal of the threat itself.

Both tree and house in the account serve as symbols of sefirot: the tree is *Tiferet*; the house, *Malkhut* (the Shekhinah), representing respectively masculine and feminine aspects of the divine. The very beginning of all movement and of creation and formation appears in the glowing mist, the divine urge to break out of its state of absolute concealment and boundlessness. The house, formed through *Tiferet*, attracts threatening forces that endanger it—the forces of impurity, the antithesis of holiness. Counteracting these forces is the worship of the divine, which effects union between *Tiferet* and *Malkhut*, and with that divine union all the seven lower sefirot glisten. *Tiferet* guards the Shekhinah, and ultimately the threatening forces of the *Sitra aḥra*—which also bring death in the world—are removed and annihilated.

Some questions may already have arisen in the reader's mind: How does the author proceed from the biblical verse about Jacob and his construction projects to this story which reflects cosmic proportions comprising the zoharic reading of the same verse? And, can this passage be properly defined as a "story"?

Approaching the first question, it is important to grasp the zoharic author's tendency to read any and every verse in a biblical text as an allusion to a deeper meaning. This meaning generally concerns the history of the higher supernal world, the creation of this world, and the drama and interaction between the two. Hence a verse from the biblical account of the life of Jacob, a verse speaking of the patriarch's constructing dwellings for his family and his animals, is here grasped as referring ultimately to the construction of the Shekhinah within the configuration of sefirot in the World of Emanation. The description comprising the zoharic interpretation of Genesis 37:17 suggests the intricate processes and modes of divine being coming into existence through emanation. The link confirming the presumed cosmic meaning of the verse from Genesis is located in the verse from Psalms (127:1), which is read as implying that any house that is built is actually built by God. If so, then in its ultimate and esoteric level the verse is grasped as speaking of an act of construction on the part of divine powers within the higher world.

A single word in the biblical verse provides a crucial key in the zoharic interpretation of that verse. The occurrence of the word *sukkot* (thatched booths) in the verse in Genesis is immediately associated with the festival of Sukkot (Booths) and with the commandment to dwell in such booths during the days of that festival along with the mystic significance of the festival and the festival booth. An entire array of associations reverberate from the word which, a non-kabbalist might assume, is employed quite innocently in a verse from the Torah relating to the work activities of Jacob. Zoharic interpretation understands the seven-day Sukkot festival as symbolizing the Seven Primordial Days that created the world, namely the seven lower *Sefirot*. Those seven sefirot (lower than *Binah*) are experienced on the seven days of the Sukkot festival.[1] These symbolic associations transform a prosaic statement in the Torah into a poetic statement of cosmic processes.

Let us turn to the second question raised concerning this passage; namely, is it a story? The Zohar's exegesis on Genesis 33:17 is, on the surface, a highly lyrical description of what is essentially recurrent. The passage includes a description of day and night, of evening twilight and the emergence of dawn—daily recurrent happenings. As such, however, the passage lacks the ingredient of time and would not follow any kind of narrative pattern.

Though the passage seems to describe what is recurrent in nature, the time factor is nevertheless present at two distinct points: the opening and the ending of the account. In its opening, the description turns to the initial divine thought or impulse to bring a world into being, to create the world of the *Sefirot* that would then serve as the inner structure of all being; thus the opening of the passage depicts the beginning point of all time. The passage concludes— again beyond the realm of the recurrent—at the endpoint of the drama of both human and cosmic history, characterized by the removal of the forces threatening the Shekhinah, the cessation of all threat to the integrity and structure of the World of Emanation, and the banishment of death from the world. Together, the beginning and the end of the passage establish a time frame that transforms the stuff of basically recurrent description into a narrative in which threat is permanently overcome and a state of wholeness is restored. The descriptive account is inscribed upon a canvas extending from the beginning point of time to its culmination and, in this sense, most clearly exemplifies what is encyclopedic in character. It encompasses the larger drama of existence that includes, even if by implication alone, the total *human* story.

The reader has probably noted the highly archetypal nature of this narrative. Its key images are distinctly cross-cultural, and it is precisely the presence of such images—it might be felt— which contributes a sense of literary power to the passage.

In numerous cultures, both the tree and the house serve as images of the universe.

While the tree in this passage refers specifically to the sefirah *Tiferet*, the tree image has different meanings in various religious traditions. It often suggests the regeneration of the universe and is also associated with the center of the universe.[2] Heinrich Zimmer refers to the "inexhaustible life-strength" that the tree represents to human awareness;[3] in contrast with the finite human life span, the tree appears, to human eyes, never to grow old or to die.[4] In the words of the biblical prophet, "For the days of My people shall be as long as the days of a tree." (Isaiah 65:22). In this connection the tree-image suggests the infinite life of the universe and serves as a symbol of immortality.[5]

The tree came to suggest an axis connecting the various worlds, its roots, trunk, and branches with their foliage serving as images of the netherworld, the earth, and the celestial worlds, respectively.[6] Not only birds but the heavenly bodies were thought to connect with the foliage of the cosmic tree.[7] And as an image of seemingly never-ending life, the tree became a symbol not only of immortality—the tree or fruit or sap of life—but of the divine as well; various trees were actually regarded as divine in nature.[8] Some early peoples perceived the universe as a tree encompassing the earth and the heavens,[9] and regarded the lights of the heavens as the fruit of the "Tree of Heaven."[10] Goblet concludes his account of the cross-cultural nature of the tree image with the suggestion that viewing the universe in the form of a tree constitutes a very natural way of thinking in traditional societies.[11]

The archetypal symbol of the tree probably came to the Zohar most directly from *Sefer habahir*, the earliest known kabbalistic text that antedates and certainly influenced the Zohar. In that text, the divine powers, situated in a hierarchy one layer above the other, are represented by the tree image.[12] In a parable found elsewhere in *Sefer habahir*,[13] a king seeks to plant a tree in his garden, and not finding a spring of water there, he first digs for a source of living water. Finding it he opens a well and then plants the tree, which is constantly nourished by the well he has dug.[14] God asserts that He planted a tree so that all would find delight in it.[15] On the cosmological nature of the tree described, an interesting passage in *Sefer habahir* speaks of the tree's twelve diagonal boundaries, suggesting the spatial and non-spatial dimensions of the cosmos that spread out to infinity. In addition, souls are situated along the tree just like birds sitting in its branches.[16]

The zoharic author states that "the Tree of Life [identified with *Tiferet*] pours forth life unceasingly into the universe" (1:131a), a life, however, that in the present state is limited due to the impact of the impure powers sometimes likened to the bark of the Tree of Emanation.[17] In another passage (Zohar 2:64b),[18] the branches of the Tree of the Holy One are said to be surrounded by twelve boundaries comprising the boundaries of the world. The tree's seventy branches are said to represent the pagan nations, whereas the people of Israel, we read, are situated in the very body of the tree.[19]

The particular description of the tree in our zoharic passage conveys a distinct sense of mystery as the tree rises above the rocks, climbing to a lofty region quite beyond human grasp and comprehension. Beyond its reference to the zoharic world-picture and its symbolism, that soaring of the tree to the region of the very highest *Sefirot* also connotes a freedom from the limitations associated with what is earthly in nature.

The image of the house, which occupies an even more central place in the passage and which specifically symbolizes the Shekhinah, also possesses archetypal resonance. In discussing archetypal patterns of imagery, Northrop Frye[20] has drawn attention to a single building or temple or stone serving as metaphor for the cosmos drawn from the mineral world, just as the world of vegetation provides for the cosmos the image of a tree.

Like the cosmic tree, the image of the House of the World is found in *Sefer habahir*. In that earlier text,[21] the image of the house is equated with the divine that transcends what is spatial in character, and referring to Proverbs 24:3 it is implied that the house is built with understanding (*Binah*). Elsewhere,[22] the author of *Sefer habahir* again focuses upon that same verse from Proverbs, "A house is built by wisdom, and is established by understanding," and notes the imperfect mode of the verb as indicating an act that is as yet incomplete. The truly significant stage of the construction of that house, of the lowest of the sefirot, the Shekhinah—it is then understood—occurs not in the past but in a future time when God will build and embellish it much beyond its present state. The unknown author of *Sefer habahir*[23] also equates Sukkot (both the festival and the place-name itself as found in Genesis 33:17) with that House which will be built by understanding (*Binah*), and he brings as a proof text the same verse from Genesis with which our Zoharic passage opens.

The very image of a house implies structure, and to the zoharic author it implies the structure of the higher worlds underlying all being including this created material world. "This house constructed the house of the world and also a world" (Zohar 1:29b). In addition to the Shekhinah, it also suggests the entire cosmos as grasped in the Zohar's world-picture; the divine powers represented more directly in the tree nourish the inner structure of all being.[24]

Still another archetypal motif emerges in the House's need for protection, as the spiritual riches, unknown and unknowable, concealed in the House entice hostile forces. In myths of various cultures, a person or dragon or animal with superhuman powers is appointed guardian of the treasures to protect them;[25] in this zoharic account God is the watchman. In another zoharic passage (2:131a, *Idra deve mashkena*), the angel Metatron is the watchman, while in 2:226b, the real watching and guarding happens in a higher place within the divine realm. Here, as with the tree and the house, the zoharic author utilizes an archetypal motif to convey, through a network of allusions, the emanation of the divine world.

Ancient temples were built to represent the cosmos; their architectural design symbolized the entire universe as understood by the ancients. This very concept, interestingly enough, is found in the Zohar itself, where "the structure of the Tabernacle corresponds to that of the heavens and the earth" (2:149a). Our passage turns this around, suggesting the converse of that thought: the totality of existence is likened to a temple, one requiring protection from defilement that threatens to violate its integrity as a holy place. A ritual, levitical model is applied to the Shekhinah and, indirectly, to the totality of the cosmos.

The model of a temple is present, within our passage, also in the role of *avodah* (worship of the divine) in fortifying the very structure of the House of the World. In his commentary, *Zohare ḥamah*, Abraham Galante pointed out that true *avodah*, consisting of both actual acts of worship together with inner devotion, rectifies the weakness within the structure. In worship, humans participate in that task of guarding and preserving the integrity of the Shekhinah, and with it, the basic divine structure that underlies all existence.

Some of the biblical verses quoted within this passage are interpreted, in classical midrashic sources, in ways that connect with the image of a temple, and those interpretations are latent in the zoharic account. In elucidating the background of Genesis 33:17 in the biblical text, a tradition recorded in *Yalkut shimoni* (1:133) explains Jacob's telling his brother Esau to continue on his way without waiting for him; Jacob's reason, we are told, is that he must occupy himself with the building of the Tabernacle and the Temple. The author or compiler of *Pirke derabbi eli'ezer* (chapter 22) reads Job 38:6-7—quoted in our passage—as the angels' singing praises following Israel's own praise to God; that reading depicts the entire universe as a vast Temple. That same effect, we might note, is captured elsewhere in the Zohar as the radiant stars sing with daybreak (1:231b) and as angels and stars together sing praises during the last third of the night extending until daybreak (1:196a).

An interpretation of Psalms 127:1 found in *Midrash tanḥuma*[26] asserts that no human was capable of setting up either the Tabernacle or the Temple of Solomon; only God could have established them. This midrashic reading interprets the word *bayit* (house) in the biblical verse from Psalms as the Temple, often referred to as *habayit* (the house).[27] The same thought is present in the zoharic author's reading of that verse as indicating that only God will construct the third Temple, and therefore it will endure, unlike the first two Temples built by human hands (3:221a).

Still another pattern from the world of ancient myth is overheard in this Zoharic passage and redefined in the idiom of the Zohar: creation is depicted as a contest between the deity who wills to create, to construct a universe, and an antagonistic force opposed to creation and structure themselves. In this passage from the Zohar, the hostile and defiling force is the *Sitra aḥra*, which emerges as a consequence of the complexities of divine emanation and of human sin; that demonic reality is manifest in the threatening spirits and armed camps described in the account. It is the *Sitra aḥra* that brings death into an existence which would otherwise be unmarred by death. The House is secure only when the *Sitra aḥra* is vanquished, and it is God who will ultimately remove the *Sitra aḥra* from the world.

It is then that the true nature of the Tree as boundless life—the nuance so central to the cosmic tree as archetype—will be realized in a world without death.

A more precise treatment, both of the narrative art and of the meanings of this highly lyrical, symbolic, and archetypal passage must consider the relationships between this account and its textual context. The text surrounding the story contains a number of motifs and themes that either echo in this account or parallel it. These come together to create a texture in which the story of the House of the World is fully integrated, placed within a landscape appropriate to its own rhythms and motifs and thematics.

Elements of this section interweave as the patriarch, Jacob, is identified as the Tree of Life (1:168a), and both are identified with the sefirah *Tiferet*. This connection provides an exegetical setting for the story.

Earlier in the zoharic exegesis on the Torah portion *Vayishlah*, it is mentioned that at the beginning of Genesis 32, the angels left Jacob alone, departing from the scene in order to chant the praises of the Holy One, blessed be He (1:166a). The theme of the chanting of prayer and praise and their role in the larger world scheme is present, assuming various forms in what precedes as well as in what follows the account of the House of the World. We read, shortly afterward, that an angel brings up the prayers of Israel and weaves of them a crown for the Holy One, blessed be He. And God, moreover, yearns for Jacob's prayer (1:167b). The prayers of the patriarchs, the text goes on to assert, sustained the world, the merit of their prayer constituting the support of both higher and lower realms. And the support that resulted from Jacob's prayer was the firmest of all (1:168a). Further into the Zohar's exegesis on this same phase of Jacob's life, the text states that when an interruption occurs in the "voice of Jacob," a break in the flow of study and prayer, the threatening "hands of Esau" become stronger (1:171a).

The Zohar's reading of events in the life of Jacob places an accent upon light and darkness, day and night. It is at night, for example, when the power of Esau is at its greatest strength (1:166a). The zoharic author identified Esau, the sibling-rival of Jacob in the biblical account and a symbol in later historical times of Rome and of Christendom which succeeded it, as a symbol of the forces of evil in the cosmos. We read that on dark nights when the light of the moon (associated with Jacob-Israel in midrashic interpretations on this portion)[28] is absent, Esau is in the ascendancy (1:169a). In his reading of the meeting of Jacob with the mysterious "man" with whom he wrestles in Genesis 32, the zoharic exegete explains that only with daybreak did the power of Esau and his dominion wane and Jacob begin to prevail (1:170b). Night is associated with exile and subjugation, whereas daybreak bestows power upon Israel who is powerless during the night of exile.

Redemption, furthermore, is symbolized by the morning light, for like the dawn, redemption will not appear suddenly in full force as a blinding light but will instead appear gradually, at first hardly noticeable and only slowly assuming dominion over the sky (1:170a). This particular complex of recurring images and ideas present within the Zohar's homilies on the life of Jacob provides a very precise context for darkness and dawn as described in the account of the House of the World.

The zoharic writer utilizes the biblical episodes comprising the account of Jacob's leaving Aram Naharayim and his returning to the land of Canaan as paradigms of conflict between the larger cosmic forces symbolized by Jacob and Esau. The paradigm of Adam and his sin repeats itself in the conflict between Jacob and his adversaries; the mysterious man with whom Jacob wrestles is identified as both the angel of Esau, the guardian angel who looks after the interests of the power of Esau-Rome, and also with Samael, the personification of evil and the demonic (1:170a). Again, preceding the story of the House of the World, we hear that Jacob's combat with the mysterious figure was a conflict with the Serpent, with the *Sitra ahra* itself (1:171a); it constitutes a parallel, on another plane, of the same cosmic conflict with the defiling force.

The episode of Dinah (Genesis 34), mentioned in the Zohar immediately following the account of the House of the World, is read as relating to the serpents who hid in order to attack Jacob (1:172b-173a). The account of the House of the World is hence situated within the zoharic text between two biblical episodes, both of which, in their zoharic reading, parallel it in their basic thrust.

The evil inclination, identified with the serpent—it is pointed out in this same section—constantly seeks to entice man and generally succeeds. Only when a person makes a special effort to strive for purification is he able to rise above the power of the *Sitra ahra* seeking to control and subjugate him (1:169a, 179a).

It becomes apparent that the real conflict described in terms of the Tree and the House is identified with an internal conflict occurring within each person. The concluding passage in the zoharic exegesis on the portion *Vayishlah* (1:179a) includes a verse from Proverbs, "The path of the righteous is like radiant sunlight, ever brightening until noon" (Proverbs 4:18). The righteous and saintly person, successfully resisting the impact of the evil inclination, is associated with the ever-brightening dawn and, by implication, enables the dawn to appear in the midst of the kingdom of night. The imagery of light and darkness is drawn from what is cyclical and recurrent, for the moral and spiritual conflict is recurrent, repeating itself in the life of each person. The same imagery, however, in the passage we have been examining, assumes a distinctly linear pattern. The pattern of ongoing conflict—our story conveys—will be broken, giving way to a condition devoid of conflict. The night of exile in human and cosmic history will be followed by the light of Redemption terminating once and for all the recurrent conflict between the holy and the demonic. At the story's culmination, the Shekhinah will be free from threat, the life force no longer limited by the fact of death, and the holiness of the supreme Temple and of all existence will be forever unmarred.

Notes

1. Zohar 2:103a, 186b; Tishby, *Mishnat hazohar* 2:521.
2. Mircea Eliade, *Myths, Rites, Symbols* 2:381.
3. Heinrich Zimmer, *Myths and Symbols in Indian Art and Civilization*, 35.
4. Ibid., 45.
5. Juan Eduardo Cirlot, *A Dictionary of Symbols*, 328.
6. Ibid.
7. Ibid., 331.
8. Eugene Goblet, *The Migration of Symbols*, 140-54.
9. Ibid., 155.
10. Ibid., 169.
11. Ibid., 171.
12. *Sefer habahir*, ed. Reuben Margaliot, 119.
13. Ibid., 23.
14. See also *Sefer habahir*, ed. R. Margaliot, 6.
15. Ibid., 22.
16. Ibid., 95 and 119; note also the analogy from English literature cited in Northrop Frye, *Anatomy of Criticism*, 144.
17. Gershom Scholem, *Major Trends*, 124.
18. Echoing *Sefer habahir*, ed. Margaliot, 95 and 98.
19. For a detailed survey of the tree as kabbalistic symbol, see Leibes, *Perakim bemillon sefer hazohar*, 107-33.

20. Frye, *Anatomy of Criticism*, 141.
21. *Sefer habahir*, ed. R. Margaliot, 14.
22. Ibid. 55.
23. Ibid. 105.
24. For a parallel to such overlapping of House and Tree, see the ancient Eridu hymn quoted in Goblet, *Migration of Symbols*, 157.
25. Cirlot, *Dictionary of Symbols*, 128.
26. *Midrash tanḥuma*, ed. S. Buber, 67a, Pekude 8.
27. Note also *Yalkut shimoni* 1:417.
28. See *Pesikta derav kahana*, ed. S. Buber, 54a.

The Sefirah of Tiferet, Beauty.

Death Postponed

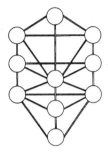

A sign of certain imminent death becomes, instead, an announcement of the deferment of death through the influence of Rabbi Simeon bar Yohai, and a father is given additional years of life in which to teach his son Torah.

One day Rabbi Isaac was sitting, extremely distressed, at the door of Rabbi Judah's house. When Rabbi Judah came out and found Rabbi Isaac sitting there in such a state, he asked him, "Why are you so different today from your usual self?"

Rabbi Isaac responded, "I came to make three requests of you: first, that whenever you will speak words of Torah that I have said, mention them in my name—for in that way my name will be remembered; second, that you will see to it that my son, Joseph, will study Torah; and third, that you will come to my graveside all seven days[1] and pray there for me.

Rabbi Judah inquired, "What makes you think your death is imminent?"

Rabbi Isaac answered, "Each night my soul ascends from me and no longer enlightens me with dreams as it did before. In addition, when I pray [the *amidah*][2] and come to the words *shome'a tefilah* [Who hears prayer],[3] though I look for my shadow on the wall I fail to see it.[4] And I can only conclude that since my shadow has departed from me and is no longer visible, an announcement must have gone forth, as it is written, 'Man walks about as a mere shadow' (Psalms 39:7)—so long as a person's shadow has not left him, his spirit is sustained within him; but once a person's shadow departs and is not seen, that person is already departing from the world."

Rabbi Judah asked him, "Where did you learn this?"

"It is written, 'Our days on earth are a shadow.'" (Job 8:9).

Rabbi Judah answered, "I will indeed fulfill all that you have asked of me, but in return I request of you to choose a place for me there[5] near your own place, just as I was near you in this world."

Rabbi Isaac cried, "I beg you; don't leave me during these days."

Together they went to Rabbi Simeon and found him studying Torah. Glancing up, the latter saw Rabbi Isaac, the Angel of Death running and dancing in front of him. Rabbi Simeon rose, took Rabbi Isaac's hand, and announced, "I decree that whoever is accustomed to enter may enter, and whoever is not accustomed to enter may not." Rabbi Isaac and Rabbi Judah came in, but the Angel of Death, bound by these words, remained outside.

Looking at Rabbi Isaac, Rabbi Simeon perceived that the sage's time had not yet arrived and that his life would in fact extend through two-thirds of the day's light. Rabbi Simeon seated his guest before him and together they studied Torah. Rabbi Simeon said to Rabbi Eleazar, his son, "Situate yourself at the doorway, and say nothing at all to whomever you may see there; and should he [the Angel of Death] wish to enter, take an oath that he may not."

Rabbi Simeon then inquired of Rabbi Isaac, "Have you seen the image of your father today? For we have learned that when a person departs from the world, his father and his close family members are there with him and he sees them and recognizes them. And similarly all those whose places in that (other) world approximate his own level gather together and are present with him, and they accompany his soul in ascending to the very place that will be his."

Rabbi Isaac responded, "Until now, I have not seen [my father's image]."

In the meantime, Rabbi Simeon rose and spoke. "Master of the World, Rabbi Isaac is known among us; he is one of the Seven Eyes[6] here. I am holding him, and I ask You to give him into my charge."

A voice was heard proclaiming, "The throne of the master is in proximity to the wings of Rabbi Simeon.[7] He is yours and he will be with you also when you yourself will enter to occupy your throne.[8]

Rabbi Simeon responded, "That will certainly be the case."

Rabbi Eleazar, noting during that time that the Angel of Death had left the scene, remarked, "There is no decree [of death] in force in the presence of Rabbi Simeon."

Rabbi Simeon asked of his son, Rabbi Eleazar, "Come here and hold Rabbi Isaac, for I see that he is frightened." Rabbi Eleazar came and held him while Rabbi Simeon proceeded to study Torah.

Rabbi Isaac fell asleep, and in his sleep, he did see his father who said to him, "My son, you have a privileged place both in this world and in the World-to-Come. For you sit among the leaves of the Tree of Life of Paradise, a large and sturdy tree in two worlds.[9] It is Rabbi Simeon bar Yohai, who is holding you in his branches. Blessed is your portion, my son."

Rabbi Isaac asked, "And what is my place there, father?"

His father answered, "For three days your chamber was hurriedly being prepared; your windows were designed to provide light for you from all four directions.[10] And rejoicing in seeing your place, I said, 'Yours is a blessed place, my son.' Until now, your son, however, has not had the privilege of studying Torah. Twelve righteous ones[11] from among the Fellows were ready to come to you. And as they were leaving, a voice stirred in both worlds: 'Who are the *haverim* [fellows] present? Place your crowns upon your head in honor of Rabbi Simeon, whose request has been granted.' Moreover, seventy places are clad with crowns here for him, with every single place opening to seventy worlds, every world opening to seventy channels, and each channel opening to seventy celestial crowns. And from there the paths open to the One who preceded all else, the One who is thoroughly unfathomable, that you might behold the celestial blessedness, the source of all light and joy, as it is said, "To gaze upon the beauty of the Lord, to frequent His temple" (Psalms 27:4).[12] What is the meaning of those words, "to frequent His temple"? It is, as written, "He is trusted throughout My household" (Numbers 12:7).[13]

Rabbi Isaac asked, "Father, how much time has been allotted me yet to live in this world?"

His father answered, "I do not have permission to tell, and furthermore such information is not relayed to those of your world. But at the great celebration[14] of Rabbi Simeon you will prepare his table, as it is said, 'O maidens of Zion, go forth and gaze upon King Solomon wearing the crown that his mother gave him on his wedding day, on his day of bliss'" (Song of Songs 3:11).[15]

Hearing these words, Rabbi Isaac awoke smiling, his face iridescent. Rabbi Simeon took note and, gazing at him, he asked, "Have you heard a joyous word?"

He answered, "Indeed I have," and reclining in the presence of Rabbi Simeon he shared with him what he had heard.

We learned that from that very day, Rabbi Isaac would take his son by the hand and begin to teach him Torah without ceasing. But when he would visit Rabbi Simeon the son would sit outside while the father would be seated before Rabbi Simeon and recite the verse, "My Lord, I am in straits; be my surety!" (Isaiah 38:14).[16]

(1:217b-218b)

Notes

1. The most intense stage of the mourning period. Jacob Moses Safrin, in *Damasek eli'ezer*, explains that during those first seven days following death the spirit still experiences distress and requires rectification. The spirit of the deceased, it was believed, returns to its house during this period immediately after death.

2. The silent devotion.

3. The blessing that concludes the requests in the *Amidah* and is said also to include all those requests (Abraham Galante, *Zohare ḥamah*).

4. The story here reflects the concept that the shadow belongs to that aspect or dimension of the soul which has been molded by the body's impact (Louis Ginzberg, *Legends* 5:108). This concept is one variation of a cross-cultural belief that views the shadow as an actual part of one's person (James Frazer, *Golden Bough* 3:77-79; Cirlot, *Dictionary of Symbols*, 43). Just preceding the story, the Zohar text mentions that during a period of thirty days before death, one's shadow is no longer visible, an idea found also in 1:227a. The same motif is expressed elsewhere in the Zohar (3:104b) in the notion that one's incomplete repentance on Yom Kippur is signified by the disappearance of his shadow. The loss of an aspect of the soul accounts for the lack of dreams during the thirty-day period before death; the phenomenon of dreams is understood as the soul temporarily leaving the body and ascending to higher realms. When this aspect of the soul has permanently parted from the body, dreams are no longer possible.

5. In the World-to-Come.

6. The seven sages who survived upon leaving the Great Holy Assembly (*Idra rabba*), Zohar 3:144a. The expression is taken from Zechariah 3:9.

7. Signifying spiritual proximity.

8. At your death. In the *Idra zuta*, Rabbi Simeon, just prior to his own death, sent for Rabbi Isaac, that the two might depart from this world together (3:287b-288a).

9. *Yesod*, the sefirah that extends from *Tiferet* to *Malkhut* and with which Rabbi Simeon is identified.

10. Channels of direct contact and blessing from the various *Sefirot* were accessible in the place assigned to Rabbi Simeon in the World-to-Come.

11. Already in Paradise.

12. In the Zohar (2:11a, 63a, 229b) this verse is interpreted as celestial bliss following death. The details concerning the sages' place in the World-to-Come allude to their ability, in that state, to experience the higher *Sefirot*.

13. The biblical verse refers to Moses. In terms of the narrative context, the verb in this verse can be understood as related to *amen*, in the sense of the acceptance of one's request in prayer. The word *bayit*, "house" or "household," also symbolizes the Shekhinah.

14. The metaphor of a *hilula*, a feast or festive celebration, for death might be traced to a talmudic parable (Shabbat 153a) in which death is likened to a banquet (*seudah*). See the following note.

15. With the death of a holy and righteous person, the learning and the deeds of the deceased during his lifetime become a force for awakening and for union within the divine, a union involving a marriage relationship between the Holy One (*Tiferet*) and the Shekhinah (*Malkhut*). Hence the death of such a person is likened to a wedding (see Safrin, *damasek eli'ezer*, Moses Cordovero, *Or hayakar*, and Galante, *Zohare hamah*). According to the last commentary, the "daughters of Zion" are the souls of the righteous, and Solomon (*Shelomo*) represents bar Yohai, who effected peace (*shalom*) in the celestial palace. Generally, the name *Shelomo* (related to *shalom*) is interpreted in reference to God (*Tanna deve eliyahu, Eliyahu rabbah*, chapter 17, page 84; *Pesikta derav kahana*, 2b, 3a). The wedding described in this verse from Song of Songs is associated in midrashic sources with the giving of the Torah at Sinai (*Vayikra rabbah* 20:10 ; *Ekha rabbati, Petihta*, 33; *Pesikta derav kahana*, 173b). Similarly, the death of a holy man is considered an occasion for revelation, a day on which one beholds even what is beyond seeing (Zohar 2:100b, *Sava de-mishpatim*), and a time of supreme, divine joy .

16. Isaiah 38:14. The significance of the context of this verse is discussed in the commentary that follows.

A story found in *Zohar hadash*, Ruth 80a-b, suggests an earlier treatment of themes similar to those found in this story. The account of the postponement of Rabbi Isaac's death might also mirror the motif in a talmudic legend of the death of King David (Shabbat 30b). In that legend, the Angel of Death is able to seize the biblical king only when the latter is distracted from his study of Torah; in our story, Rabbi Isaac is granted additional years in order to teach Torah to his young son.

Commentary

"Death Postponed" closes with a quotation from Isaiah 38:14, "My Lord, I am in straits; be my surety," words which, in the biblical source, appear in the context of the illness and healing of Hezekiah, king of Judah. This closing quotation is a convenient point at which to begin an examination of the story. On the surface the words would not seem to convey anything crucial to the narrative; they evoke, however, in the mind of the author and of his readers, the biblical episode where they appear, and the tradition of interpretation associated with it.

According to the aggadic expansion of Hezekiah's illness and recovery as found in *Pirke derabbi eli'ezer*, chapter 52, Hezekiah's experience is cited as the very first example of recovery from illness since the world began. As such, his trial serves as a prototype of recovery. While our story from the Zohar makes no mention of illness in connection with Rabbi Isaac, it does share with the biblical sources the motif of the postponement of death, since fifteen years, it is reported, were added to the life of the biblical king (II Kings 20:6; Isaiah 38:5).

The words from Isaiah placed in the mouth of Rabbi Isaac were spoken as part of Hezekiah's prayer following his close encounter with death and his recovery. The medieval exegete Rashi paraphrased the biblical king's prayer of thanksgiving, "You have taken me from the hand (the jurisdiction) of the Angel of Death and have secured my safety." Even after the body of the zoharic story has already been told, the presence of but a fragment of a biblical verse contributes to the story a dimension of depth; in its wake, the narrative comes to mirror Scripture, and the postponement of Rabbi Isaac's death is grasped as an overtone of the biblical source.

In addition to the motifs of recovery and the prolongation of life after a divine decree of imminent death, the biblical source (and its parallel, II Kings 20: 8-11) makes mention of a sign—a change in the position of the shadow on the balcony steps—given to the king from

God. The alteration of the shadow from its normal place at that particular moment signifies the nullification of the death decree and the king's recovery (Isaiah 38:7-8). Though the precise nature of the sign is different, in the zoharic story the reader also notes that the shadow serves as a sign relating to life and death.

In a further expansion of the biblical accounts of Hezekiah's illness and healing, a talmudic passage in the name of Rabbi Yohanan (Eruvin 26a) states that during the king's infirmity, the prophet Isaiah conducted Torah study at the door of the king's chamber. The talmudic source goes on to mention the possibility that Torah study at the doorway of the room of an ill person might unduly antagonize Satan (the Angel of Death); Rashi, in his commentary, however, suggests that precisely because of the gathering of students for study at the doorway of the scholar-king, the Angel of Death did not have permission to enter into the room.

An entire complex of motifs—including those of the doorway and the Angel of Death—from the biblical episode and from its expansion in talmudic and other aggadic sources are present in the zoharic story of the near-death of Rabbi Isaac. The reader might reasonably locate the genesis of this particular zoharic story precisely in that tradition, biblical and postbiblical, concerning King Hezekiah. The same motifs—the postponement of death, the shadow as sign relating to life and death, the doorway, and the Angel of Death—are interwoven to form a new and very different configuration in the zoharic narrative.

We have not, however, exhausted the points of connection between the zoharic narrative and the episode concerning King Hezekiah in the Bible and in postbiblical tradition.

The history of the near-death of Rabbi Isaac flows from a quasi-narrative discussion recounting the happenings, unknown to a dying person, that precede his death. Following the story the same discussion resumes, focusing primarily upon what happens to the soul following the moment of death. While some of this discussion continues in a semi-narrative descriptive vein and includes also a rather brief anecdotal story, the text in some places is clearly homiletical in character.

Rabbi Hiyya inquired, "What is the meaning of the verse, 'He will destroy death forever'?" (Isaiah 25:8). Rabbi Simeon said, "When the

Holy One, blessed be He, arouses His power [His Right Hand],
death will be made void from the world, but He will not arouse His
Right Hand except through Israel's awakening the Right Hand of the
Holy One, blessed be He, and how is that done? Through Torah
study, as it is written, 'Lightning flashing (*esh-dat*, "fire of law") at
them from His right'" (Deuteronomy 33:2). [Zohar 1:219b]

The homily goes on to discuss the proclamations, in Paradise or
in Gehenna, for the righteous and the evil person (*ra*), respectively,
thirty days prior to death. The latter—through midrashic textual
methods, including the transposition of the order of letters in a
word—is identified with the one who, in sexual intercourse, "spills his
seed upon the ground" as did Er (Genesis 38:9). This act intrinsically
and singularly negates the opportunity of repentance, for it is tanta-
mount, the homily declares, to the murder of one's own children.[1]

The story and the nonnarrative content of this homily echo each
other in a remarkable convergence of themes. In the story, Rabbi
Isaac's death is postponed explicitly in order to enable him to teach
his son; the son, in this sense, spares the father from death. On a
broader plane, bringing children into this world allows for the possibility of their pursuit of Torah study, which in turn will negate death
for the whole world. And the sin of the king, Hezekiah, which had
brought on his illness—later mentioned in this same portion of the
Zohar—involved his refusal to marry and have children, whereas following his healing and repentance, he did take a wife (1:228a-b).

This assertion in the Zohar text relates to the theme found in a
talmudic reading of the Hezekiah scenario (Berakhot 10a). There
Isaiah is said to have explained to the stricken King Hezekiah that his
death has been decreed on high for the reason that he did not make
an effort to establish a family, "to be fruitful and increase" (Genesis
1:28). The king explains his reason for not doing so in his having
foreseen that his descendants would not be worthy. After the prophet
instructs the king that his obligation was to do what had been commanded, leaving what follows to God, Hezekiah asks to marry the
prophet's daughter. Isaiah, however, refuses, for the decree had
already been proclaimed. (An older version of the talmudic text adds
that Hezekiah does indeed marry Isaiah's daughter, after which
Menassah was born to the couple.)[2] The presence of this very theme

in a talmudic passage relating to Hezekiah points to an even deeper significance to the Hezekiah tradition and its complex of motifs as a source of this story in the Zohar.

"Death Postponed" opens as Rabbi Isaac is sitting at the door of his fellow sage's house. The setting of a doorway, mentioned, as we have observed, in a talmudic aggadah relating to the illness of King Hezekiah, reverberates at various points throughout the story. Rabbi Simeon, noting the Angel of Death running and dancing in front of Rabbi Isaac, decrees that whoever is not accustomed to come to his house (i.e., the Angel of Death) may not enter, and the Angel of Death consequently remains outside. Rabbi Simeon then orders his son to situate himself at the doorway, lest the Angel of Death enter. The doorway motif echoes also at the very end of the story when the reader is told that when Rabbi Isaac would thereafter visit Rabbi Simeon to study with him, his young son, who is now studying Torah on his own level, would sit outside. Both the repeated mention and the oblique presence of the doorway as a metonym in the text appear, on one level, to allude to the figurative gateway separating life from death. The narrative as a whole, in this sense, has its setting at that doorway between life and death, and looming over the events in the story is the question: will the sage be allowed *not* to pass through that doorway even after having experienced those signs of imminent death?

The same figure of the doorway also reflects another kind of meaning in terms of the symbolism that pervades the Zohar. The "opening" refers to the lowest of the *Sefirot*, the Shekhinah, which is an opening, and the only opening, to the higher *Sefirot*. And with death comes a moment of disclosure in which the dying person, just before the Angel of Death actually appears, sees the Shekhinah, perceiving what one is unable to see until this dying moment. In the story, though Rabbi Isaac's death is postponed, he is nevertheless privy to the kind of vision and knowledge beyond that accessible to mortals prior to their death.

An emphasis upon the act of seeing is present at various points within the discussions surrounding the story in the Zohar text. The dying person is able to see his relatives and friends who are already deceased (1:218b); in addition, in tracing the stations of the soul following death, the soul, at a certain point, is able to see the "Presence and majesty of the King" and to experience the celestial joy of that vision (1:219a).

This ability to perceive what is intrinsically unseen is reflected also in the repeated occurrences of verbs indicating sight within the story. The Aramaic root *hami* (observe, see) appears twelve times within the course of the narrative passage, and in addition the root *hazi* (see, recognize) appears twice. During prayer Rabbi Isaac is unable to see his shadow. Rabbi Simeon is able to see that Rabbi Isaac hasn't quite reached his moment of death. Rabbi Eleazar is instructed to say nothing to whomever he saw at the doorway. Rabbi Simeon, in his prayer of pleading, refers to Rabbi Isaac as one of the "Seven Eyes." Later, Rabbi Simeon perceives that Rabbi Isaac is in a state of fear. Approaching the very end of the account, Rabbi Simeon looks at Rabbi Isaac and finds him smiling, his face iridescent. Two biblical verses (Psalms 27:4; Song of Songs 3:11) interwoven into the text of the story intensify the leitmotif of seeing; they contain, respectively, the Hebrew verbs *hazah* and *ra'ah* (see), referring, in this context, to the bliss experienced in the World-to-Come.

The reiteration of words expressing the act and capacity of seeing serves to focus emphasis upon the moment of revelation that immediately precedes death, and upon the climactic example of seeing in the story: Rabbi Simeon inquires of Rabbi Isaac whether he had yet seen the image of his father (in a vision) that day—this being a sure sign and prerequisite of imminent death. Paradoxically, when that sign of certain death later occurs, it becomes instead an announcement of the postponement of death, the turning point in the plot around which the story revolves.

The motif of the deceased father's appearing to his dying son exemplifies an ongoing code implicit in various ways within the narrative account: the negation of aloneness in death. At the beginning of the story, Rabbi Isaac begs his companion not to leave him; the thought of dying alone intensifies his dread of death. That very fear, that in death a person experiences an uncompromising aloneness, is then negated by the sense of community that accompanies death in the story. In the discourse following the story, the author quotes the tradition that at the hour of a person's departure from the world, his deceased father, his other family members, and others with whom he had associated in life gather around him and accompany his soul to its abode (Zohar 1:218b), just as those already in Paradise leave their places there to visit the dying person. The bonds among the *ḥaverim*, members of a circle engaged in the study of mystic wisdom, forge a fellowship that endures into the life beyond death. Death, moreover, is described as a great feast or festivity (*hilula rabbah*), a social situation. And Rabbi Judah counters Rabbi Isaac's requests with one of his own: that he and Rabbi Isaac might be together in the other world as they have been in this world. The emphasis on togetherness embodies the antithesis of the presumed loneliness in death, which, one might claim, continues to loom psychologically in the background of all its negations.

It is highly suggestive that the man standing on the threshold of death is accompanied by a young son. The role of the son in the story recalls the archetypal figure of the child signifying rejuvenation,[3] in this case a new lease on life given the sage who is living in the very shadow of death. The child-figure symbolizes youth in contrast to age, a proximity to birth in contrast to the approach of death. The child's presence in this story, moreover, suggests a sense of continuity even in the face of death; the archetypal connotation of the child is given a specifically Jewish value/function in focusing upon the commandment given to the father to teach his son Torah (Kiddushin 29a).

Having observed some aspects of the narrative art in this story, including a striking example of intertextuality, let us proceed to the kinds of relationships connecting this story with its own textual context.

In both the zoharic homilies on the preceding Torah portion, *Vayigash*, and the brief section of the Zohar on the portion, *Vayeḥi*, that precedes this story, the reader notes two significant subjects of direct relevance to the story. One is the glorification of Rabbi Simeon bar Yohai; the other is the subject of death and the power over death.

Concerning the first, it is stated that in creation, God founded the world upon a single pillar, "the Righteous One," which maintains the very existence of the world and also sustains the world (1:208a). In zoharic symbolism, "the Righteous" alludes to the sefirah *Yesod*, with which Rabbi Simeon bar Yohai is identified. The early part of the Zohar on *Vayeḥi*, preceding our story, goes on to include an elegiac account of the aftermath of the death of bar Yohai. In a dream, bar Yohai soars upward together with a Torah scroll and many books until he, and the writings, are lost from view; with his death wisdom has vanished from the world (1:217a).

The theme of Jacob's psychological revival, following word that his son Joseph is yet alive ("the spirit of their father, Jacob, revived," Genesis 45:27; Zohar 1:206b; 1:216b) recurs in the Zohar text following the story (1:225b); in the latter statement of this theme, Joseph as the *Yesod*, the "foundation" of the world, connects implicitly with Rabbi Simeon bar Yohai, just as his father, Jacob, in bed and about to die, parallels in this sense the situation of Rabbi Isaac in the story.

The biblical King David, according to the Zohar text, exemplifies a measure of power over death. It is reported that he always avoided sleeping the length of time necessary to experience the foretaste of death, the dream-state in which the soul temporarily leaves the body; David was thoroughly attached to the Side of Life, the life-quality in the kabbalistic cosmos, rather than to that of death (1:207a), and his cleaving to God made for life (1:207b, based on Deuteronomy 4:4).

Within the textual context of the story, Elijah is also mentioned in a similar connection. First, the prophet complains that the tree of death had been given dominion over the widow (I Kings, chapter 17) whom God ordered to sustain the prophet (1:208b). Elijah notes that over several years the Angel of Death had failed in pursuing him, because the prophet, too, had attached himself to the Tree of Life. Elijah, we are told, was born with unusual vitality and, for this reason, he did not experience death as do other human beings but was instead transformed into an angel (1:209a). In addition—and this is significant for the story—God tells Elijah that the latter had "already completely closed the gate in order to guarantee that death would not come to him" (1:209a-b). In order to connect the motif of Elijah's never having died with the tradition linking him with the commandment of circumcision and with his actual presence at every rite of circumcision, it is explained that due to Elijah's zeal for God the Angel of Death was given no power over him (1:209b). Elijah is also mentioned immediately prior to the background-setting of the story of Rabbi Isaac's encounter with death (1:217a).

These two thematic strands, the praise of bar Yohai and the avoidance of or power over death, merge together in the story. It is bar Yohai, in our story, who is shown to possess a significant degree of power over death, having an influence in the higher worlds that he exercises on behalf of his friend who is about to die. Bar Yohai, in this way, is placed alongside David and Elijah among those reported to have power over death.

The account of Rabbi Isaac's deferred death is in some ways quite inconsistent with the tenor and thoughts voiced in the background passage immediately preceding it. This passage depicts a human being as totally unaware of the signals and message announcing his death. A human being, it is said there, "neither sees nor hears nor knows" the signs and the voice that proclaim his death. The passage quotes the verse, "(Such things had never been heard or noted.) No eye has seen, O God, but Yours / Who act for those who trust in You" (Isaiah 64:3), as a proof text for a person's inability to detect the signs of approaching death. The story qualifies that lack of knowledge on the part of a human being. It focuses upon the subtle signs by which a person can nevertheless know that his death is imminent. Among these is the lack of a shadow, a clear indication that one's death will occur within a thirty-day period. The story proceeds directly from this statement concerning the disappearance of one's shadow during the period prior to death. The background passage's mention of two birds (angelic beings) who transmit the celestial proclamation of death and who are themselves trapped in the darkness suggests that death is a trap from which there is no escape. The decree bears a clear sense of finality: beyond the time designated for one's death, "one's days cannot be prolonged."

Yet, unlike the lyrical discourse's image of the birds trapped in the void, in the story death is not a inescapable trap; even Rabbi Isaac's loss of his shadow does not necessitate the irreversible conclusion that he is about to cross the very threshold of death. The initial sense of man as a powerless victim of the death process is seriously qualified by the kind of influence in the higher worlds that the narrative ascribes to Rabbi Simeon bar Yohai. The proclamation of one's death in the celestial worlds, described in the background passage, contrasts with another announcement, that of the acceptance of Rabbi Simeon's request. The story constitutes the antithesis of the overall tenor of the same background passage that occasions it, and that antithetical relationship accentuates both the limitations of death's jurisdiction and the role of Rabbi Simeon as a protagonist having spiritual power over death.

If the father's as-yet-unfulfilled vocation of teaching his son Torah constitutes a prime factor in the postponement of Rabbi Isaac's death, it complements, as another factor, the spiritual power of Rabbi Simeon bar Yohai. On one level he is ultimately the central figure of the story, which exemplifies the genre of the *shevah*, the legend told in praise of a holy personage. Unlike some folk tales in which the hero conducts a contest with the Angel of Death by tricking him,[4] there is no element of trickery in this story. It is, instead, the purely spiritual influence of Rabbi Simeon bar Yohai within the larger cosmic vista that makes possible the postponement of Rabbi Isaac's death.

Rabbi Simeon's role is the direct antithesis of that of the Angel of Death, and the emerging polarity points to a reading of the story as mirroring the more total zoharic story. The postponement of death in the narrative signifies that death, identified in zoharic Kabbalah as a consequence of the demonic, is not invincible. On this level, bar Yohai represents the forces of holiness destined to triumph over the demonic. With redemption, death will utterly vanish from the world. According to the Zohar (1:164a), the complete realization of monotheism will be marked by an end of death itself. The narrative imagination of the author could qualify the power of death precisely because of the faith that death is not ultimate but will, in its time, be vanquished from the world and from the worlds. As is the case with other narratives in the Zohar, an infinitely larger cosmic story, identical with the Zohar as a whole, radiates from this narrative of the post-ponement of Rabbi Isaac's death.

Notes

1. In Genesis 38:9, it is Er's brother Onan who is guilty of this act. Er's sin, while meeting with God's emphatic disapproval, is not explained (Genesis 38:7). Rabbinic sources, however, identified Er's sin with that of Onan (Yebamot 34b; *Bereshit rabbah,* 85:4).
2. Louis Ginzberg, *Legends,* 6:370 n. 94.
3. C. G. Jung and K. Kerenyi, *Essays on a Science of Mythology,* 83-84; Juan Eduardo Cirlot, *A Dictionary of Symbols,* 43. 4. Stith Thompson, R.185.1, "A Mortal Deceives the Angel of Death".

The Sefirah of Netzah, Victory

The Bridegroom's Silence

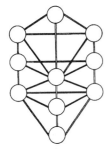

A bridegroom who, out of humility, feigns ignorance, is later seen to be a brilliant interpreter of the Torah.

At midnight, while staying at an inn, two sages were discussing the importance of Torah study; upon overhearing them, a daughter and her father, the innkeeper, both broke into tears. The father then explained to his guests that their weeping had to do with his having given his daughter in marriage to a young man lacking all knowledge of Torah. He went on to explain how it happened that he had selected such a man to be his daughter's husband.

"One day I saw him as he leaped from a tall roof simply in order to hear the *Kaddish*[1] recited in a congregation. At that very moment I decided to give my daughter to him, and I proceeded to do so just as soon as people had left the synagogue. For I felt that his eagerness in leaping for the purpose of hearing the *Kaddish* was a clear sign that he was a person of marked ability and potential greatness in Torah study. And even though he was still a youth, and though I hadn't known him prior to that moment, I nevertheless chose him.

"But now, it turns out, he does not know even the very simplest things such as the Blessing after Meals,[2] and I cannot study with him among the *ḥaverim* that he might learn even to recite the *Shema*"[3] or the Blessing after Meals."

[Rabbi Yose] remarked to the bride's father, "Exchange him for another, or, if not, perhaps [at least] he'll have a son who will turn out to be a master of Torah."

While they were still talking, the bridegroom appeared and rose, leaping to take a seat in front of them. Pondering him, Rabbi Yose declared, "I detect in this young man that either from him or from a son who will be born to him the light of Torah will definitely radiate to the world."

Smiling, the young man asked, "My masters, allow me to say a few words in your presence." And he began, "I am young of days, whereas all of you are older than I am. For this reason therefore I was too awestruck and fearful to hold forth among you" (Job 32:5-6).

[He went on to describe Elihu[4]—whose words from Job those were—as having come from a family background of considerable honor, the family of Ram,[5] and ultimately of Abraham[6] and a priest and a descendent of the prophet Ezekiel, too. Nevertheless, Elihu remained silent for a considerable length of time while his elders first spoke their words.][7]

"I, too, had said, 'Let age speak; let advanced years declare wise things. But truly it is the spirit in men, the breath of *Shaddai*[8] that gives them understanding' (Job 32:7-8). Therefore precisely because I am young, I, too, had decided not to speak, at least until two months had passed. Today marks the completion of that two-month period. And now that you are present, allow me to speak words of Torah in your presence."

He began [and referred to the Primordial Light,[9] which] "though it is destined to bear fruit in the World-to-Come, also even now every day if not for this light, the world would not be able to exist . . . as it says, 'A light is sown' (Psalms 97:11)— continuously sown.

"My masters, I am from Babylonia and am the son of Rabbi Safra, though I was not privileged to know my father. I left home and, in voluntary exile, came here. And I so revered those living in the Land[10] here as lions of Torah[11] that I considered it disrespectful to speak words of Torah in anyone's presence for a period of two months. Now that those two months have passed, I am privileged that you have come here this day."

Rabbi Yose cried aloud, and all those present rose before the young man and kissed him on his head. Rabbi Yose exclaimed, "It is our good and blessed lot that we chanced to come this way and have heard from your mouth words of the One who has preceded all else, words which, until now, we had never been privileged to hear."

When all were seated, he addressed them. "My masters," he said, "I saw the anguish of my father-in-law and of his daughter who were placed in a distressful situation and experienced such depth of sorrow because I did not know even the Blessing after Meals. And consequently, I was unwilling to have intimate relations with my wife as is customary until I would comprehend the full meaning of the Blessing after Meals, even though there would have been no sin in our marital relationship. I did not wish to cause them displeasure, and yet at the same time I could not speak and disclose my knowledge until these two months had passed."

Both Rabbi Yose and Rabbi Hiyya along with the youth's father-in-law and his daughter all rejoiced, even to the point of weeping from such intense joy. Rabbi Yose requested, "Please, since you are now permitted to speak, brighten and enlighten our day. Blessed is our lot in coming this way and in our being present here."

The youth began, expounding first on the subject of the Blessing after Meals. [He then went on to interpret the meal as a sacred occasion and the Blessing after Meals as a joyous event, as he explained the mystic meaning of the components of that series of blessings.]

In the meantime, dawn had come up, and all those present rose from their places and kissed him.

Rabbi Yose announced, "This is indeed a festive day, a true wedding celebration, and we shall not depart from here until a wedding celebration and feast takes place with all the townspeople in attendance. This is a celebration willed by the Holy One, blessed be He." They blessed his wife, reciting numerous blessings; they furthermore arranged that her father prepare the house as befitting the joyous occasion, and they gathered all the townspeople for the celebration and made the bride happy. They continued to rejoice with them that entire day, and with his words of Torah the bridegroom, on his part, contributed to the gladness of the occasion. When all were seated around the table, again he began to teach Torah [explaining that at the occasion of a wedding one must prepare for the bride a beautifully decorated canopy as a way of giving honor to the celestial Bride[12] who is present at the wedding, having come to share in the joy of the bride. And similarly, he explained, when the bride is blessed with the Seven Blessings at her wedding, so is the Shekhinah, the celestial Bride, blessed with those Seven Blessings corresponding to the seven lower *Sefirot* of the Godhead].

That entire day they rejoiced with words of Torah and the townspeople all appointed him as their leader. The next day, Rabbi Yose and Rabbi Hiyya rose and blessed the couple before proceeding on their way to visit Rabbi Simeon.

When they arrived, Rabbi Simeon looked up, taking note of them, and he told them, "I saw you today, and I saw you during the two days and the night that you were in the Tabernacle of that lad, Metatron,[13] and this lad, Metatron, taught you celestial mysteries in the joyous mood of Torah study. You were indeed privileged that this be your lot, my sons."

They shared with Rabbi Simeon all that had occurred. He then remarked to them, "You are privileged as I, too, am privileged, for I recall one day when I was walking along the road with his father, Rav Safra. And as we were about to part, I blessed him that he might have a son who would be a Lion of Torah learning, but I did not make a point of blessing him that he might know his son. Yours is a privileged lot, my sons, and concerning you it is written, 'And all your children shall be disciples of the Lord'" (Isaiah 54:13).

(2:166a-169b)

Notes

1. Prayer for sanctifying the Name of God. This prayer, which is recited only in the presence of a *minyan*, a quorum of ten, includes a response on the part of the congregation, and the lad leaped to be able to join in the congregational response.

2. *Birkat hamazon.*

3. Three paragraphs from the Torah (Deuteronomy 6:4-9; 11:13-21; Numbers 15:37-41), which, in daily Jewish worship, are recited morning and evening.

4. His words are found in Job, chapters 32-37, following the speeches of Job's three friends and Job's response to their words.

5. "High, exulted."

6. In various sources, Elihu ben Berakhel is identified with Isaac (Jerusalem Talmud Sotah 5, 20d; *Yalkut shimoni* 2:918) or as a son or grandson of Buz, nephew of Abraham, or son of Nahor, Abraham's brother (*Yelamdenu* in *Yalkut shimoni* 1:766; *Sekhel tov* 70 on Genesis 22:21; *Targum* on Job 32:32). Ezekiel's father's name was Buzi and was a priest (*kohen*) (Ezekiel 1:3).

7. Among the traits said to characterize a wise person, a passage in Mishnah Avot (5:9) mentions one's refraining from speaking in the presence of one who is greater in wisdom and learning.

8. A name for God.

9. According to rabbinical lore, God withdrew the Primordial light

created on the first day of creation when man sinned; according to tradition, this light is preserved for the righteous in the World-to-Come.

10. The Land of Israel.

11. In a similar vein, Rabbi Zera, upon coming to the land of Israel from Babylonia, fasted a hundred times in order to forget the learning he had previously acquired in Babylonia (Baba Metsiah 85a).

12. The Shekhinah.

13. The angel who presides over the celestial Tabernacle (Zohar 2:143a; 159a). He is mentioned also as the head of the celestial academy (Zohar 3:186a), and this association is central to his mention in the story. According to a source in *Bamidbar rabbah* 12:12, he offers, in the celestial Tabernacle, the souls of the righteous as an atonement for Israel during the days of their exile when the Temple sacrifices do not exist. He is referred to as "the lad" and, in the source in *Bamidbar rabbah*, is identified with "the lad" mentioned in Exodus 24:4 and I Samuel 2:13.

Commentary

Perhaps more so than in any of the other zoharic stories in this collection, the reader recognizes in "The Bridegroom's Silence" the patterns of a conventional folktale. Yet after a more comprehensive examination, this same tale can be seen to reflect elements close to the very core of the zoharic ethos and of its particular grasp of the nature of being.

The sequence of events in the story has three stages, each with its distinct image of the bridegroom and his Torah knowledge or the lack thereof. First comes the father's initial impression upon which he hastily acts, a perception that appears afterward, in the second stage, to be grossly incorrect, bringing regret and deep distress. The third stage, surprisingly, confirms the validity of the father's initial impression. The first and second stages are told by the bride's father, and the story is acted out before the reader or listener only when the second stage is about to conclude and the third begin. At this turning point, the bridegroom leaps just as he is about to confirm his bride's father's initial interpretation of his first leap. Between these stages, objective reality itself does not change; what changes is the accuracy of the perceptions of that reality.

In his commentary on the events recounted to him, Rabbi Simeon adds to the story a fourth stage as the bridegroom and his knowledge are now seen to occupy an even more exalted level. The bridegroom is identified with the angel Metatron, the lad translated into angelic form who presides over the halls of Torah in the higher realms and who reveals knowledge of Torah to human beings in this world. The word *na'ar* (youth) appears early in the story in reference to the bridegroom, ironically as a term of potential derision; at the end, that same term explicitly connects with *hana'ar metatron*, "the lad, Metatron," and with his very exalted status in the higher world. Rabbi Simeon knows and reveals the true identity of the disguised figure. That disclosure casts in an even more ironic light the responses of those within the story's second stage who were unable to grasp the nature of the lad's true identity, relating instead only to his disguise.

When the story begins, a bride and her father weep upon over-hearing the scholarly conversation of two sages staying at an inn. The emotional tenor of this account shifts, in the course of the story, from weeping to joy, a joy expressed through its own kind of tears. The weeping and bitter disappointment at the beginning allow for a deeper and even more intense joy at the end. These emotions, coloring the narrative, are not unrelated to discussions in the text of the Zohar preceding the story.

Insisting upon the imperative of joy in the service of God, the author considers the dilemma of a person simply unable to rejoice due to trouble or sorrow. The author responds by stating that "the gates of tears are never locked" (2:165a).[1] A more complex and para-doxical answer to the same question, however, emerges in the form of the story itself. Sadness, in the tale, is grasped as the consequence of a deception, as a veil placed over the truth of things, whereas true reality, when disclosed, evokes joy.

The story serves, on one level, as a narrative frame for the homiletic or ideational content located within the frame, and the reader immediately notes certain threads making for a heightened integration between the story and the bridegroom's discourse within the story. The bridegroom's apparent ignorance in the story is exemplified by his inability to learn even the *birkat hamazon*, the prayer of thanksgiving following a meal. That inability was, of course, a deception on his part and yet not totally a deception, as he refused to recite the *birkat hamazon* until he had first grasped its complete meaning including the mystic significance of that prayer. A considerable portion of his discourse during the wedding feast focuses upon the *birkat hamazon* in the specific form in which it is recited during the wedding feast. In his discourse, he interpreted the *birkat hamazon* with the Seven Blessings (added at the wedding feast) as an occasion of profound joy in the world of the divine. Further integration between the frame story and its homiletic content is evidenced in the discussion, within the discourse, of the wedding and its practices, a subject obviously connected with the wedding of the bride and bridegroom in the story.

If the story serves as a framing narrative for an extended discourse within the Zohar text, that same discourse, in turn, serves as the thematic context of the story itself. The discourse provides an insight into the significance of the story in which a mystic-sage, for a certain length of time, conceals the fact of his erudition and his powers of interpretation. During his discourse, the bridegroom focused upon the *or haganuz*, the Hidden Primordial Light, which, according to rabbinical exegesis on the opening verses of Genesis, was withdrawn and concealed for the righteous in the World-to-Come. That concept of the Hidden Light, signifying a more sublime and complete consciousness—a concept we will discuss further on at greater length—is reflected within the story in the concealed state of the bridegroom's knowledge.

———————————————————————————

A much more impressive degree of integration is noted when the story is seen in its larger context within the homilies comprising the zoharic exegesis of the Torah portion *Terumah*. Specific themes and subjects are emphasized and recur and also interconnect within those same homilies. These include sadness and joy, the Tabernacle and Temple as scene of a supernal bridal canopy, the Song of Songs, the *shema'*, *birkat hamazon*, the real nature of Torah, wine as a symbol of joy, the bride and the bridegroom, hiddenness, Metatron, and the union or unity of the divine and of all existence. Together, these themes and concepts reverberate in the story which follows.

The shema', with its note of oneness (*eḥad*, "one"), is explained as the occasion of union between masculine and feminine forces within the Godhead, between *Tiferet* and *Malkhut* (the Shekhinah); the reciting of the *shema'*, we are told, effects such union and unification within the realm that underlies all being (2:160b). At the same time, the *shema'* connects with the Seven Blessings recited after the wedding feast, for in the context of those wedding blessings the Shekhinah, the Supernal Bride, blesses that person who has recited the *shema'* and, in doing so, has brought about union in the higher realms (2:161a). And the second verse of the *shema'* (*ve'ahavta*, "You shall love the Lord your God," Deuteronomy 6:5),we read, points to the mystery of the Primordial Light (2:162b).

A discussion revolving around the symbolic situation of "eating at the King's table" leads, in the Zohar, to the consideration of Deuteronomy 8:10, the Toraitic proof text for the Blessing after Meals (2:153a). Giving thanks during the *birkat hamazon*, we are told, makes for joy within the higher realms (2:153b). Furthermore, the obligation to recite the *birkat hamazon* even outside of the Land of Israel connects with the Holy of Holies in the Temple, once the dwelling place of the Shekhinah (2:157b).

Torah is defined, within that body of zoharic teaching, as the knowledge of the Oneness of the higher and lower levels within the divine realm (2:161b); the study of Torah kindles a light which emanates from the Primordial Light itself (2:166a-b). Within the directions for building the Tabernacle in the wilderness, Moses was shown Metatron, because the latter would be ministering to Michael, the High Priest, within that Higher Tabernacle called by his name (2:159a); further into the text, "the lad, Metatron" is identified as the watchman or guardian of the Tabernacle (2:164a).

A passage within these same pages ascribes the theme of hiddenness to the opening verses of the Song of Songs; a veiled subject ("Let him kiss me with the kisses of his mouth," 1:2) conveys that the ultimate levels of the divine are unknowable, beyond the reach of human cognition (2:146b). The Primordial Light is similarly hidden, though even in its hidden state it brings forth light by means of the *tsadikim*, the righteous and saintly (2:147b). In discussing various kinds of gold, the text mentions the "higher gold" beyond the reach of the human eye (3:148a). The Hidden Light, it is later explained, is hidden as is a seed in the ground, which then germinates and produces life (2:148b); though itself hidden, it is the force that renews creation (2:149a).[2] And the Primordial Light itself is a High Priest in the celestial Tabernacle situated even higher than that of Metatron (2:159a). Further approaching the story, we read that the Shekhinah is concealed in the faces of *tsadikim* (2:163b).

Joy is a prerequisite to approach the seventh of the firmaments, *aravot*, and for this reason the High Priest was required to enter the Holy of Holies in a joyous mood (2:165a). Similarly, the blessing over the cup of wine used in connection with the Blessing after Meals and the Seven Blessings must be recited in a joyous mood (2:168b). In explicating the opening verses of the Song of Songs, the zoharic author refers to the light proceeding from the aged, preserved wine symbolizing both the supreme joy and the Divine Name (2:147a). Both in discussing the Tabernacle and in describing the human body and the mystery of the human person the author accentuates the theme of union; each is a union embracing many individual parts—in the latter case—a union of male and female (2:162b).

Even from such a skeletal outline of the themes and topics found in the Zohar text preceding this story, one grasps the degree to which the story serves as a collective resonance of that entire complex of thematics and motifs. What might have appeared as a rather simple and not unconventional tale is consequently seen as reflecting a host of concepts peculiar to the spirituality of the Zohar.

In homiletic statements made by Rabbi Yose and Rabbi Hiyya at the inn prior to the crying of the bride and her father (2:166a-b), discussion centers around the Oral Torah and the Written Torah, the former receiving its light from the latter. The Oral Torah is associated with the Shekhinah (*Malkhut*), the basically feminine sefirah, while the Written Torah symbolizes *Tiferet*, the essentially masculine sefirah within the constellation of forms of the Divine Being. The text interprets the verse from Psalms (97:11), "light is *sown* for the righteous," as suggesting a sexual relationship, and the event of revelation at Sinai is similarly expressed in terms of union of the masculine and feminine forces within the Divine: "The sin of the First Man was healed only at the event of revelation at Mount Sinai as the lamp and the light [Oral and Written Torah, *Malkhut* and *Tiferet*] joined in union" (2:168a). In the light of this nonnarrative, homiletical passage preceding the story, the marriage scene in the story acquires a distinctly symbolic dimension. Associated with the sefirah, *Tiferet*, is the conception of the emergence of articulated speech within the course of the emanation of the sefiriotic world; the transition in which hidden thought gives way to language might well be reflected in the bridegroom's vow of silence, which is then followed by his words of Torah.[3]

Acquiring additional dimensions of meaning from the network of themes that precedes the narrative, the wedding in the story symbolizes and partakes of a greater, all-inclusive union and oneness—a cosmic or "sacred marriage" within the divine and, through it, involving all of being. That wedding is an occasion of joy, total joy in the higher realms, a mirth refracted throughout all of existence. Similarly, that sadness occurring in the second stage of the story reflects an infinitely vaster sadness, flowing from the very lack of union above. It reflects a state of nonmarriage on a cosmic plane. It is therefore appropriate that the bridegroom refrained from engaging in marital relations during that sixty-day period, for without Torah study, without the *birkat hamazon* and without the reciting of the *shema'*—concerning which he feigned ignorance—the higher union, the celestial marriage, does not occur. The celebration of the marriage in the story coincides with sadness giving way to the greater divine joy.

Upon rereading the story after noting the ideational texture of its broader context, one can grasp more clearly the lad's leap from the roof to hear the *Kaddish*. The *Kaddish* is recited only in the presence of a *minyan*, a quorum of ten Jews, and while the Zohar represents prayer as effecting a harmonious relationship among the *Sefirot*—specifically the union of *Tiferet* and the Shekhinah (the Supernal Bride among the sefirot) and the repair of the Shekhinah within the World of Emanation (2:216b)—the act of prayer is claimed to have greater import when it occurs in a *minyan* (3:126a). Furthermore, the very word *Kaddish* can connote *kiddushin* ("marriage"), a word of the same root. The kaddish symbolically foreshadows the later *Kiddushin* in the story.

The bridegroom's disguised state, his illusory lack of Torah knowledge, similarly acquires deeper meaning in light of the thematic strands of the zoharic homilies on the portion *Terumah*. It reflects the sense that all flows from what is intrinsically hidden and is dependent upon what is unknown and unknowable. And Torah, specifically, emanates from that hidden region identified with the Concealed and Primordial Light.

The later disclosure of the bridegroom's true nature and of his erudition and brilliant mystic insights, furthermore, parallels what is stated in a passage from the text preceding the story: while the full meaning of Solomon's Song of Songs was hidden even from the sages of earlier generations, it was disclosed through Rabbi Simeon bar Yohai in his generation (2:149a). The disclosure of the bridegroom's learning parallels the disclosure of the teachings of the Zohar itself!

Some basic connections implicit within the story become clearer when we recall that the hidden Primordial Light is said to be located in the sefirah *yesod*.[4] And it is precisely this sefirah that makes possible the union of the masculine and feminine dimensions of the Divine, that higher union which is symbolized, on a human level, by marriage and the wedding. Seen in this light, the significance of the wedding theme in this story become markedly clearer.

The Hidden Light connects, in the story, with the motif of the incognito sage, a motif found also in other stories from the Zohar. Within the Zohar's homiletic exegesis on *Terumah* a few pages after the story, the reader encounters a story concerning Rav Huna [II, 174b] who, like the bridegroom in our story, came to the Land of Israel from Babylonia. Initially the students in the academy pay no attention to him, for he is young and they do not know him. Ultimately, however, when they become aware of the extent and depth of his knowledge, he comes to earn their respect. This little story of Rav Huna echoes the more developed narrative of the "Bridegroom's Silence"; both stories focus upon a young Torah scholar whose youth served as a disguise, a cloak concealing his knowledge and insight. This association recalls the figure of the *yanuka*, the child-scholar, who is deceptive in that he possesses a knowledge and understanding that belie his youthful appearance.

This general pattern recalls still other stories from the zoharic literature in which a person feigns ignorance—a person whom none would suspect of possessing any significant knowledge but who goes on to impart mystic teaching that amazes his listeners with its insight and brilliance. Several examples immediately come to mind:

In one such account (2:94b, *Sava de-mishpatim*), an old porter whom Rabbi Yose meets along the road plagues him with constant questions that sound to his ears like empty chatter. The porter maintains his ignorance in matters of Torah and, on the surface, his conversation seems to lack all sense. He goes on, however, to explain one of his seemingly foolish questions with a learned and original discourse on the subject of the journey of the soul as an interpretation of some of the Torah's civil precepts. Rabbi Simeon bar Yohai later informs Rabbi Yose and his colleague that they had been in the presence of a supreme Lion of Wisdom with whom not even the greatest sages can compare (2:111a).

In a somewhat similar story, a thirsty man begging for water along the road explains, when asked, that he is familiar with the Torah only through a son for whom he has acquired a teacher. This same man insists on being told a question that had perplexed the sages he met along the road. "Sometimes in the undergarment of a poor man one finds a jewel," he remarks, going on to offer an impressive resolution of the problem that they most reluctantly posed. The stranger turns out to be a leading scholar of mystic teaching from Babylonia who has been consistently unwilling to reveal his identity as a scholar (3:157b-158a).

In still another passage in the zoharic literature, the reader encounters similar stories about a *yanuka*, whose understanding in this case extends beyond erudition to a knowledge of the deeds of others. While the child adamantly refuses to disclose his identity, Rabbi Simeon bar Yohai does so, adding enigmatically, "He will not be known in the world, because there is in him something of an exceedingly high nature" (3:186b-192a, *Yanuka*).

These stories recall motifs found in other sources telling of persons who, clandestinely, perform compassionate deeds. In the Zohar, however, this story pattern assumes a much more specific direction, that of the (temporarily) incognito sage or master of mystic exegesis. The immediate effect of this motif is the creation of a setting in which the highest wisdom is prevalent and found even in the most unexpected quarters.

This story type of the incognito sage reflects a basic aspect of the zoharic mind and its grasp of reality, one that has already surfaced in our discussion of this narrative. A recurrent dialectic between hiddenness and disclosure is present throughout the Zohar. The ultimate dimensions of being and of the Godhead, the source of all that is, are situated in the realm of the unknowable, quite beyond the reach of the human mind. The same is true of the ultimate layer of the soul, the supernal soul, "the soul of all souls, inscrutable and never disclosed, unknowable, though everything is dependent upon it" (1:254a). The revealed and the known have their source in what is hidden.

This same dialectic, we might suggest, is a definite though subtle factor in the shaping of innumerable stories and legends from a later period, stories telling of the *tsadik nistar*, the incognito holy man whose true qualities, knowledge, and spiritual power are hidden from the world. This type of story came to assume a highly significant place in the folk culture of Ashkenazic Jewry.[5]

In the later folkloristic motif, the *nistar* is said to belong to a clandestine class of incognito holy persons. Many tales point to the premise that it is of the nature of the highest level of holiness to be concealed from the eyes of the world. This motif merges with the much older idea that the world is sustained by a specific number of righteous people, usually thirty-six,[6] as these righteous came to be identified with the incognito holy men of whom human society is unaware. In such stories, the incognito figure intentionally conceals his identity and his knowledge and permanently maintains a hidden state as a matter of principle. The disclosure of his identity as a *tsadik* often requires that he mysteriously vanish from the scene or, in some of the later tales, depart from the world.[7]

Such tales tell of the incognito master of mystical Torah who inevitably assumes some kind of mask that deceives the world concerning his real nature. Sometimes he appears grossly physical, lacking any intellectual dimension to his life. Sometimes he performs the simplest tasks for a livelihood and exhibits lowly conduct, lacking all normal social graces. He might be bizarre in his appearance or mannerism or character, and even appear outwardly to follow a lifestyle remote from even the most basic of traditional Jewish values. Through such masks, the concealed mystic fully hides his knowledge of Kabbalah and his real level of spiritual power.[8] And in these tales the incognito holy man—like the Hidden Primordial Light—plays a crucial and indispensable role in the very continuation of the world's existence.

The type of the *tsadik nistar* known from later folklore is not found in the Zohar and differs in pronounced ways from the type of temporary anonymity exemplified in "The Bridegroom's Silence." The very definite contrast between the two has suggested the possibility that the later concept of the *tsadik nistar* might be the result of extraneous influence.[9] Yehuda Leibes,[10] however, has suggested that the basis of the *tsadik nistar* concept, so popular in eighteenth century Jewish lore, is actually present in the Zohar in reference to the figure of Rabbi Simeon bar Yohai, who is identified with the sefirah *Yesod*: the *tsadik* is the foundation (*yesod*) of the world (Proverbs 10:25) who sustains the world even while he himself is concealed—likened to that sefirah which is symbolized by the male sexual organ. According to Leibes, this idea, implicit in the Zohar, may have blossomed in the eighteenth century through the influence of popular preachers who found in this zoharic concept a rationalization of their own situation as clandestine followers of the seventeenth-century messianic figure Sabbatai Zevi. Taking a different tack, Daniel Matt[11] has suggested the possibility that the extolling of the hidden and of anonymity in the Zohar might relate to Moses de Leon's concealing his own authorship of the Zohar.

Both the later stories of the incognito *tsadikim* and the temporarily incognito mystic-sage of the zoharic stories, including "The Bridegroom's Silence," appear to mirror a basic "cultural code" or underlying ethos. On the level of the narrative and the folk tale they mirror one nuance of the underlying sense of reality characterizing the major traditions of Jewish mysticism.

Within the nonnarrative content of the Zohar, the reader finds the kind of statement that appears to approach the core-premise of the motif of the incognito holy man, in particular as it developed in later centuries. Commenting upon the words of Kohelet, "Then I accounted those who died long since more fortunate than those who are still living, and happier than either are those who have not yet come into being" (Ecclesiastes 4:2-3), the zoharic author explains that "best of all is the one who has not separated from God and is *concealed in obscurity*, the pious saintly ones who observe the precepts of the Torah and study the Torah day and night; such a person attains to a level higher than that of all other people" (3:183a; italics mine).

Notes

1. Baba Metsiah 59a.
2. Mircea Eliade, writing on the religious traditions and philosophies of India, refers to a transcultural concept of the creative power of light (*Myths, Rites, Symbols: A Mircea Eliade Reader* 2:328). On the sense of the procreative power of light in Indian as well as Buddhist and Gnostic traditions, see Eliade, *History of Religions* 2:1-30, "Spirit, Light and Seed."
3. See Gershom Scholem, *Two Treatises by Rabbi Moses de Leon*, p. 335; M. Idel, "Reification of Language in Jewish Mysticism," p. 61.
4. See 1:45b and also 2:166b-167a, cited above, where the relationship is implied through reference to Psalms 97:11.
5. See Gershom Scholem, "The Tradition of the Thirty-Six Hidden Just Men."
6. On the number of such righteous said to live in each generation, see Moshe Ber, "*Lemekorotav shel hamispar lamed-vav tsadikim.*"
7. See several of the tales included in Mordecai Ben-Yehezkel, *Sefer hama'asiyot* 2:7-82.
8. Several tales exemplifying the *tsadik nistar* motif were collected by Ben-Yehezkel in his *Sefer hama'asiyot* and also in Israel Klapholz, *Lamed-vav tsadikim nistarim*. See also Gedaliah Nigal, *Hasiporet haḥasidit, toldoteha venoseha*, 252-63.
9. Rudolf Mach, *Der Zaddik in Talmud und Midrasch*, 134-46, has suggested that the later Jewish folk-motif of a clandestine class of concealed holy persons could be a Judaization of a concept found in the lore and thought of Islamic mysticism and evident in Sufi and Shiite sources. Mach refers in particular (138) to the *abdāl*, ranks of holy men (and women) who are said to live unrecognized among people but whose influences contribute to the maintenance of the world order. He points (139) to the idea of the hierarchy of four thousand, unknown both to the world and to one another, part of a larger hierarchy headed by the two *Imāme*. According to Mach (142), this Islamic concept, which views the *tsadikim* as pillars of the world, maintaining its order, recalls earlier rabbinic description of the *tsadik* and of the patriarchs as pillars and also as mountains, protecting the dry land from the sea's flooding. Henri Corbin (*Histoire de la Philosophie Islamique*, 300-301), in discussing the thought of Sohrawardî, mentions the sages who excel both in philosophy and in spiritual experience and who live an incognito existence as does the Imam at the summit of that mystic hierarchy. Seyyed

Hossein Nasr (*Three Muslim Sages*, 111) describes those sages as outwardly resembling other people but as having realized in their own being all the potential universal qualities and human possibilities. Gill and Kramers, in their *Shorter Encyclopedia of Islam*, 55, refer to an eleventh-century concept that the cosmic order is preserved by a fixed number of saints, so that when a holy man dies his place is immediately filled by another. The number of such sages varies in different sources, ranging from seven to three hundred.

10. Yehuda Leibes, *Hamashiah shel hazohar*, 14, nn. 209 and 211.

11. Daniel Matt, *Zohar: The Book of Enlightenment*, 30.

The Sefirah of Hod, Splendor.

A Retelling of Jonah

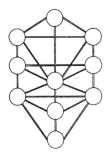

The biblical story of Jonah is read as a parable of human experience from birth through death to resurrection and renewed life.

A parable of the life of a human being in this world:

Jonah, who boarded a ship,[1] is really the human soul[2] who descends to this world in order to enter into the body of the person. Why is it called Jonah (denoting torment)?[3] Because together with the body it experiences agony and affliction in this world, as it is said, "Do not wrong (afflict) one another" (Leviticus 25:17). A person living in this world is like a ship in danger of being shattered in the midst of the Great Sea, as it is said, "the ship was in danger of breaking up" (Jonah 1:4).[4] And when a human being sins in this world, he thinks of fleeing from the presence of his master rather than giving thought to that other world.

But the Holy One, blessed be He, sends forth a strong storm wind, the person's judgment continually in God's sight and pursuing its execution. The storm strikes the ship and directs attention to the sins of that person that he may be seized. By means of that storm the person is taken through illness, as it is written, "he lay down and fell asleep" (Jonah 1:5). But even though a person is afflicted with illness, his soul is still not moved to return to its Master that it might be redeemed from its sins. What is written? "The captain went over to him and cried out" (Jonah 1:6).

Who is the captain? The good inclination which is in a position of authority. And it says to him, "How can you sleep so soundly! Up, call upon your God" (Jonah 1:6). This is not a time for sleep, rather it is the time to present yourself for judgment concerning all that you have done in this world; repent of your sin. Consider these things and return to your Master:

"What is your business?" With what did you occupy yourself in this world? Confess concerning it before your Master. "Where have you come from?" (Jonah 1:8) Consider from where you have come— from a putrid drop[5]—and you will not feel proud in His presence. "What is your country?" (Jonah 1:8) Consider that "from dust you were created, and to dust you will return" (Genesis 3:19). "And of what people are you?" (Jonah 1:8) Consider whether or not you have merit from your fathers which can come to your defense. Since you are about to be called for judgment before the heavenly court, this storm, which is a judgment-decree raging against you, voices a demand of the King, seeking to judge His prisoners. All His counselors appear before Him one by one.

It is then that the court is formed. Some speak in the person's defense while others press for conviction. And the court insists that justice be done. If the person is not acquitted, what is written? "Nevertheless, the men rowed hard to regain the shore, but they could not" (Jonah 1:3)—those who speak on his behalf strive with great effort to restore him to this world, but they are unable to do so. Why? "For the sea was growing more and more stormy about them" (Jonah 1:13). The judgment of guilt rages with greater and greater force due to the person's sins until it prevails over him.[6]

As is proper, three messengers are appointed to bring evidence against him. One has a written account containing both all the meritorious deeds and all the transgressions that he had performed in this world; another has a reckoning of his days, and the third is the one who has accompanied him from the time that he was still in his mother's womb. It becomes clear that the demand for judgment for his sins is not appeased until, as it is written, "they heaved Jonah overboard" (Jonah 1:15). "And they heaved": they took him from his home to the gravesite, in accordance with the proclamations concerning him. If he is innocent, it is proclaimed concerning him, "Give honor to the image of the King." "Yet he shall come to peace, he shall have rest on his couch who walked straightforward" (Isaiah 57:2). From where? As it is written, "Your Vindicator shall march before you, the Presence of the Lord shall be your guard" (Isaiah 58:8). But should he be found guilty, these proclamations are heard concerning him: "Woe to this person; it would have been preferable for him never to have been created." It is written, "And they heaved

Jonah overboard, and the sea stopped raging" (Jonah 1:15).

When they brought him into the graveyard following the judgment, the decree of judgment that had been raging now calmed from its fury. The fish that swallowed him is really the grave: What is written? "And Jonah remained in the fish's belly" (Jonah 2:1). The belly of this fish is actually the belly of *She'ol.*⁷ On what basis is this identity established? It is written, "From the belly of *She'ol* I cried out" (Jonah 2:3). And should it otherwise be understood simply as the belly of the fish and nothing more, it is here clearly written, "the belly of the Netherworld."

"Three days and three nights" (Jonah 2:1)—these are the three days during which a person lies in the grave with his inward parts split open. After those three days, the stomach's filth is poured out upon his face as the body declares to him, "Take what you have given me. For you ate and drank all day long without ever giving to the unfortunate, and all of your days were as festive days while the poor were famished, never eating with you; therefore, take what you have given me!" This is as it is written: "I will strew dung upon your faces (the dung of your festival sacrifices, and you shall be carried out to his [heap])" (Malachi 2:3).⁸

In this way it is confirmed that during the span of time following those three days, a person is afflicted in his eyes and in his hands and his legs, the pain continuing for a period of thirty days. During all those thirty days the spirit and the body together receive punishment as one entity and for this reason the soul remains present below, beneath the ground, and does not ascend to its own place, like a woman who dwells apart during all the days of her impurity.⁹ Afterward when the soul ascends, the body decomposes in the ground until that time that the Holy One, blessed be He, will awaken the dead.

A voice will then resound among the graves, announcing, "Awake and shout for joy, you who dwell in the dust! For Your dew is like the dew on fresh growth; You make the land of the shades come to life (You will cast down the land of the shades)" (Isaiah 26:19). When will this occur? At the time that the Angel of Death will be removed from the world, as it is written, "He will destroy death forever" (Isaiah 25:8).¹⁰ Since He will have swallowed death for all time, it then follows that "My Lord God will wipe the tears away from all faces and will put an end to the reproach of His people" (Isaiah 25:8). And concerning this it is written, "The Lord commanded the fish, and it spewed Jonah out upon the dry land" (Jonah 2:11).

Immediately when that voice will be heard among the graves, each grave will cast forth the dead which it holds, as it is written, "You will make the land of the shades (*refa'im*) come to life" (Isaiah 26:19).[11] What are *refa'im*? The dead will experience healing, restoring them to their former condition, bone to bone, and so these are called *refa'im* (*rfa*, "heal"). And if you say, it is written (in connection with idolaters), "[they are] shades, they can never rise" (Isaiah 26:14), certainly all the world will find healing in the grave. But some will rise, whereas others will not. And it is concerning the latter that it is written "[they are] shades, they can never rise." But Israel will have a good destiny, as it is written concerning them, "My dead bodies shall arise" (Isaiah 29:19).

In the account of the fish one finds words of healing for all the world, for upon swallowing Jonah the fish died, but after Jonah was inside the fish for three days, the fish was restored to life and cast out Jonah, as it is written, "Jonah prayed to the Lord his God from the belly of the fish" (Jonah 2:2). It is written here *dagah*[12] and it is similarly written *dagah* in another verse, "and the fish in the Nile died" (Exodus 7:21); just as there the fish died, so here too, the fish had died. The land of Israel is similarly destined to be stirred to new life, and following that, all "the earth will cast forth its dead" (Isaiah 26:19).

(II, 199ab)

Notes

1. Hebrew idiom for boarding a ship, literally "went down to a ship."

2. Also in *Tikkune zohar* (a later strand of zoharic literature) 21, 53a, the soul is referred to as *yonah* (Jonah). The name means "dove," and Cordovero, in *Or hayakar, Vayakhel* on Zohar 2:199a, explains that the soul, facing the dangers of life and of judgment and death, is like a dove who thinks it can flee from the storm.

3. Cordovero, in *Or hayakar, Vayakhel*, commenting on this passage, suggests that the soul is called *yonah* from the word meaning "tormented" or

"oppressed," as the soul is tormented within the body. Having come from and belonging to the celestial world, it naturally seeks to ascend to its own place but, counter to its own nature, is forced by God to exist in a material world.

4. Cordovero, in *Or hayakar*, observes that whereas formerly the word for ship is *sefinah*, here the word *aniyah* is used, connoting a weaker vessel made of less sturdy materials.

5. Mishnah Avot 3:1.

6. Or, over those who speak in his defense.

7. The Netherworld.

8. In Shabbat 151b and in *Vayikra rabbah* 18:1, the same verse is read in a similar way, referring to the stomach's bursting on the third day after death.

9. Leviticus 18:19.

10. In *Kohelet rabbah* 1:4, this verse is understood as God's annulling (healing) the distinction between the celestial creatures and the earthly creatures who are subject to death.

11. Understood as "the earth will cast out the *refa'im.*"

12. Feminine form of *dag* (fish).

Commentary

A zoharic exegesis on a biblical text generally relates to single verses, even to specific words of a biblical text, and rarely to an entire episode or narrative. In contrast, this particular passage of zoharic exegesis stands out as a running, extended commentary on two entire chapters of the Bible, the first two chapters of the book of Jonah. In his homiletic exegesis on these chapters from Jonah, a narrative text, the zoharic author—it would appear—has actually created a new and very different story, a parable of human experience extending from the soul's entry into the body to God's awakening the dead at that time when death will be no more.

The Zohar's allegorical reading of Jonah[1] is constructed upon certain suggestions within the biblical text. For instance, the verb *yrd* ("to go down," Jonah 1:3) appears in the beginning of that text in the idiomatic sense of boarding a ship; that same expression, however, to the Zohar's author, suggests descent itself, the ultimate descent, that of the soul which leaves the higher worlds in order to inhabit this physical world. Jonah's lying down in the ship (Jonah 1:5) suggests a state of illness. And the occurrence of the word *She'ol* ("the netherworld," Jonah 2:3), conveying a state of near death, becomes a prooftext for the exegete's identifying the fish with the grave and with the state of death itself.

Some elements in the parable suggest contemporary influences upon the zoharic author. The description of the ship "in danger of breaking up" (Jonah 1:4) suggests the body that ultimately succumbs to the storms and stresses of life. This kind of association is likely drawn from the cultural landscape of Spanish and Provençal Jewry: in his *Behinot olam*, the thirteenth-century Hebrew poet Berdisi (Yeda'yah Hapnini) of Provence likens the world to a raging sea and the human body to an inn for the soul, one which, employing the same biblical phrase, is "in danger of breaking up."[2] The image of the pilot and ship, which denote soul and body respectively, was current in medieval Spanish literature and in European medieval writing generally, in works highlighting the contrast between body and soul and especially in debates between body and soul.[3] Descriptions of the body's decomposition are found in the body-soul dialogues prevalent in medieval Spain, both in Latin works and in writings in the Spanish vernacular.[4]

Several passages in the zoharic literature display a distinct attraction to the sea. These include a highly rhapsodic description of a storm at sea followed by calm waters (2:48b). Elsewhere an old sage, struggling with the interpretation of a biblical text, likens himself to a sailor rowing against a powerful current but determined to prevail; later, he compares his satisfactory counter of challenges to this interpretation to escaping with his life from the raging waves (2:98b; 100b, *Sava de-mishpatim*). And in an another passage, the preexistent soul of Moses is described as having descended to the world "in one of the boats which sail on that great Sea" (2:54a).

In zoharic symbolism, the sea often represents the tenth *Sefirot*, *Malkhut*, which is also a recipient of the forces of judgment from the higher *Sefirot*; elsewhere in the Zohar (1:121a) the sea in Jonah represents the Divine Throne as a force of judgment. While in other contexts the sea, as well as the fish and storm, serve as Kabbalistic symbols, the homiletic exegesis in this passage lacks any direct reference to what is specifically theosophical in nature, to the hidden life-processes within the divine, the world of sefirot and their emanation. Exemplifying *remez* (allusion to allegorical meaning) rather than *sod* (allusion to Kabbalistic mysteries), it is closer, in this respect, to the allegorical interpretation typically found in *Midrash hane'elam*, the very earliest strata of the Zohar, or to the allegorical readings in the writings of the followers of Maimonides, such as Jacob Anatoli's collection of sermons, *Malmad hatalmidim*. Such allegorical interpretations tends to translate the elements of a text into a conceptual pattern in which the real protagonists are body and soul, form and matter, or good and evil inclinations.

In contrast with such philosophical allegory, the Zohar's exegesis on Jonah substitutes a story for a story. It reads the biblical narrative not as a code for an abstract statement but rather as the larger, universal story of every human being. And in the Zohar's narrative re-creation of Jonah, one significant note is heard that—while not flowing from a specific zoharic theosophy—displays themes which distinctly transcend the aura of philosophical allegorical interpretation.

The zoharic author reads the second chapter of Jonah—and through it the story as a whole—as a parable or typology of death and resurrection. Furthermore, the pattern of death and resurrection is given multiple expression in the zoharic retelling of the Jonah story. Having identified the fish with the grave and with *She'ol*, the zoharic exegete grasps Jonah's departure from the fish as the dead leaving their graves and their state of death. In the same passage, the word *refa'im* from Isaiah 26:19, understood as the dead, is explained also in terms of the root *rfa* ("heal"). "What are *refa'im?* The dead will experience recovery and restoration to their former condition, bone to bone, and so these are called *refa'im*." Whether a twisting of a word in the biblical text, or an example of close reading on the part of the zoharic author, the word for shades (spirits of the dead) is made to convey both that the dead will be healed, that death involves healing, and that death paradoxically serves as a gateway to renewed life. The Zohar weaves into the story the motif of the fish's death upon swallowing Jonah and later its restoration to life, a reading based upon the use of both *dag* and *dagah*, masculine and feminine forms, respectively, of the noun "fish" within the text (Jonah 2:2). This reading, found in at least one other thirteenth-century source,[5] exemplifies the themes of death and resurrection in different elements of the Zohar's reading of Jonah.

The Zohar's commentary and retelling of Jonah is part of a long *derush* (homiletic composition) on Exodus 35:5: "Take from among you gifts to the Lord, everyone whose heart so moves him shall bring them—gifts for the Lord" (The words "take from you," *kehu me'itkhem*, can be read also as "take of yourselves"), and mention is made in the homily of one's becoming, as it were, an offering to the Lord. The *derush* focuses upon the journey of the soul, following death, through its various ordeals of judgment and purification until it finds its place in a celestial realm of being. Apart from the Jonah scenario, nowhere in that entire *derush* is resurrection mentioned. This detail raises the question of the Zohar's relationship to the concept of *tehiat hametim* (Resurrection of the Dead) and to its grasp of the concept more as a symbol of the annihilation of death than as bodily resurrection itself.[6]

In other ways, however, the Zohar's retelling of Jonah definitely echoes in the *derush* of which it is a part. The journey of the soul, the ascent that diametrically parallels its former descent to this world, is mapped out in complex detail comprising a very definite body of zoharic mythology. The stations of the soul's journey purify it of its sins and also of the physical quality it acquired through its descent to this world and its attachment to the body (2:211b). In place of its body and its garments, dimensions previously given to the soul to enable it to exist in a material world, the soul receives celestial garments of a distinctly spiritual nature (2:210b). In this case, the Zohar's dualism of body and soul leaves no room for mention of bodily resurrection.

In its discussion of the liturgy of morning worship, the subject that occupies a considerable part of the *derush*, the *nefilat apayim* ("falling on one's face" during *tahanun*, the prayer of penitence), is understood as an offering of one's soul (2:200b). Among the basic principles of prayer is the worshipper's "surrendering his soul" to God with a wholeness of readiness and intent (2:202b). Hence, the death depicted in the Zohar's reading of Jonah reverberates in an interpretation of daily worship as including an act of symbolic death. A parallel to death is seen in the departure at night of one's soul, which leaves this world to ascend and return to the higher realms from which it came (2:213b).

The soul descends to this world ("goes down to that ship") to ascend later to another plane of being, more exulted and sublime. Similarly prayer, uttered with true devotion, ascends to the higher world (2:201b). With the coming of the Sabbath, the additional soul, associated with the Shekhinah, descends as a heavenly guest to this world; later, at the Sabbath's close, it ascends once again (2:207a; 208b). In this way, various themes and movements of descent and ascent mirror one another throughout the *derush*.

The dew, mentioned in Isaiah 26:19 and quoted within the Jonah scenario, is also mentioned in what follows, not in connection with the restoration of the dead to life in a renewed physical existence—as in midrashic exegesis on the vision of the Valley of Dry Bones[7]—but rather with the healing of the soul following the ordeals of its journey after parting from the body. After having bathed in a river of fire (*nehar dinur*), the souls go on to immerse themselves in the healing dew that comes from the letters of the Torah engraved in the heavens (2:210a).

The pattern of death and rebirth to new life, the basic underlying rhythm of the zoharic Jonah passage, echoes most significantly at the very end of the lengthy *derush*. Here the journey of the soul is described: during the sleep of night, the soul leaves the body, which remains like inert stone; we are told that the souls of the righteous and devout ascend to a higher realm, where they form a crown for the Holy One, to Whom they are then offered as a sacrifice. Note here the connection with the biblical verse to which the entire homily relates (Exodus 35:5). With this act of sacrifice, the soul, with all its deeds and Torah-learning, is absorbed within the Supreme Point, which reconceives it as a mother so that the soul emerges reborn (2:213b).

In this way, the zoharic author explains the freshness and renewal experienced in the morning as the soul's rebirth within the celestial realm—specifically within *Binah*, the divine womb—after a nightly death experience. The *derush* ends with this parallel to its reading of Jonah in which death is followed by renewal and the ultimate annihilation of death.

The zoharic homily, with its restatement of Jonah, does not exist in isolation from the homilies preceding and following it within the zoharic exegesis on the Torah portion *Vayakhel*. In the homily that directly precedes it, several strands are present which later echo in the reading of Jonah. All people, we read in that earlier homily, experience a kind of death each night in that their souls leave their bodies and ascend to the upper worlds, and the phenomenon of dreams is explained in connection with that nightly ascent of the soul when it leaves the body (2:195b). Mention follows of the Angel of Death and the days on which he has permission to inflict harm and effect judgment (2:196a). The subject of death and the Angel of Death continues in that homily with the claim that the mixed multitude which accompanied the Israelites upon leaving Egypt brought down the Angel of Death to the world (2:197a).

This homily then turns to the subject of Elijah, the early biblical prophet, and relates the verse, "Who has ascended to heaven and descended?" (Proverbs 30:4) to both him and to Jonah. In response, it is pointed out that Elijah ascended to heaven, while Jonah descended to the deepest levels of the sea. The homily points both to parallels between Elijah and Jonah and to contrasts between them (2:197a). Shortly afterward, Jonah is again mentioned as the example of the kind of stipulations that God made with what He had created on each of the days of Creation (2:198a). When, in the very next *derush*, the zoharic author turns at length to his reading of Jonah, the ground has been well-prepared for his subject.

The very last part of the zoharic exegesis on the Torah portion *Vayakhel*, following the homily that includes the Zohar's retelling of Jonah, raises the subject of the death of the Serpent—identified as the demonic forces in the cosmos, the *Sitra aḥra*, and hence also as the Angel of Death and the Evil Inclination.[8] With the death of the Serpent, we read, the deceased will awaken and live as part of the ensuing messianic scenario. At this point in the text, resurrection is explicitly mentioned: the dead will form throngs in the Galilee as each person so restored marches to his ancestral area of land. Clad in special garments, they will then make the ascent to Jerusalem to offer thanksgiving (2:220a). The concept of resurrection, though not occurring elsewhere within the homily containing the Zohar's retelling of Jonah, nevertheless reverberates here toward the very end of the zoharic exegesis on *Vayakhel;* the retelling of Jonah echoes at considerable distance from its own place in the text of the Zohar.

The biblical book of Jonah consists of four chapters; the zoharic exegesis relates only to the first two, concluding as the fish casts out Jonah onto the dry land. It would appear from this passage that the book concludes at midpoint, prior to Jonah's experiences in Nineveh relating to the real possibility of repentance and upon God's acceptance of the repentant sinner. *Pirke derabbi eli'ezer,* the earliest work that relates to Jonah as an extended narrative, similarly includes a retelling of chapters 1 and 2 in the context of a discussion of the sea animals created on the fifth day of creation. The rendition of Jonah in that passage (chapter 10 in the printed edition) does not go on to treat the latter half of the biblical text. That same source, however—considered to date from the eighth century—includes elsewhere (chapter 43), in a very different context, a retelling of the events of the latter two chapters of Jonah.

The Zohar's focus in the exegetical passage under discussion is shaped in its entirety by the first half of the Jonah story. While elsewhere in the Zohar repentance is certainly accentuated, it is clear that in this passage the zoharic author's interest in Jonah is located not in that concept but elsewhere.

The Zohar often gives expression to aspects of mythic imagination that traverse cultural and religious borders, and the zoharic author reads Jonah through the lens of what is essential to the mythic impulse. For close to the very core of myth, going back to ancient Egyptian and Mesopotamian lore and beyond, is the formula of a god's death and resurrected life giving promise to his/her believers that the connection with life is not broken by death, that death is but one side of a coin, the other side being renewed life.[9]

Bringing together both death and resurrection in a single scenario, the zoharic reading of Jonah brings all the resonance of mythic imagination to bear upon the concept of the Resurrection of the Dead, a core concept of classical rabbinical thought. This re-creation of the Jonah story is one of a number of stories in the Zohar which ultimately interpret death as a nondeath, stories reflecting the belief that death itself will vanish from the world as the holy and pulsating divine life will become liberated from demonic threat and influence.

We began with the suggestion that the Zohar, in its interpretation, creates of the biblical book of Jonah a new story. More precisely, however, it may actually recreate something of the effect of a much older story. The folk tales paralleling that of Jonah and the fish in various cultures point to the possibility that the biblical author, directly or indirectly, drew from such an older tradition while utilizing it for his own distinct purposes.[10] Almost a century ago, William Simpson,[11] citing numerous parallels, posited that the first half of the Jonah story grew out of an older legend of initiation that simulated death and rebirth. Of considerably greater significance than Simpson's precise conclusion, related to the older theories of myth and ritual, is his accumulation of a large number of parallels to the Jonah story from diverse sources that nevertheless share a common tendency to exemplify themes of death and rebirth.

Considerably closer to our own time, Mircea Eliade[12] and others have interpreted the fish in the Jonah story and its analogues in other written and oral literatures as symbols of death; the hero who is swallowed by a fish or animal is undergoing a deathlike experience; that experience, it is suggested, corresponds in its larger context to the chaos preceding new creation, the death signaling new life. The sea, furthermore, is said to connote both the grave and the womb; it is the scene both of death and rebirth.[13] Simpson,[14] for example, pointed to the expression *mibeten she'ol* (Jonah 2:3), literally "the belly of the netherworld," as suggesting the womb.

That same deathlike experience of Jonah within the fish is also, in some sense, an experience of birth. Maud Bodkin has suggested that the precise choice of words in this biblical text evokes a rhythm suggesting a deeper archetypal pattern of death and rebirth.[15] In Jonah's prayer in the second chapter, the subject's experience of "near death" is expressed in imagery evoking the actual experience of death itself. In addition to the reference to *She'ol*, note the word *shahat* (Jonah 2:7), a word understood in other biblical passages (Psalms 30:10, Job 33:24) as a grave.

It is interesting to note, further, that in some Islamic retellings of the Jonah story, the prophet—when cast out of the fish—is described as a "newborn" or even as a "small chicken without feathers."[16] Jonah, it is related, is ejected from the fish "like an infant wrapped in swaddling clothes."[17]

James Ackerman[18] has found in both the language of the Jonah story and in the imagery of Jonah's prayer overtones of a deathlike state, a steady descent toward death and a subconscious will to die. These overtones are expressed, among other ways, in Jonah's going down to the ship's hold and in his deep sleep there, as well as in his sojourn inside the fish. Ackerman has suggested that the verb *veyera-dem* ("and he fell into a deep sleep," Jonah 1:5) in the text echoes the recurring root *yrd* (to descend). Jonah's deep sleep exemplifies his going down toward death, a dormant act symbolizing the quest for death.

In Jonah's three days and nights inside the huge fish, George M. Landes[19] has detected echoes of an old mythological motif of the time required to traverse the distance from the world of the dead, a motif first expressed in that particular verbal stamp in a Sumerian myth, "The Descent of Inanna to the Nether World." It would appear that the death imagery utilized as metaphor in the biblical text of Jonah surpasses the role of metaphor and becomes real in the Zohar's reading of Jonah.

Shalom Spiegel[20] also refers to the span of three days as a familiar time formula, the time required by Tammuz, Osiris, and other gods to descend to and return from the netherworld. Quoting Von Baudissin, Spiegel[21] further suggests that this concept, in turn, might reflect the days of darkness at the end of the lunar month, followed by the reemergence of the moon's light. In his exegesis on Jonah, the zoharic author may be making explicit some of the more subtle nuances of this pattern of death and the overcoming of death, a pattern that modern students of myth and folklore as well as of the biblical text have recognized in the Jonah story and in stories similar to it. In his reading and metamorphosis of Jonah, the zoharic author may have succeeded in detecting overtones of the archetypal substratum of the biblical book.[22]

We might then proceed to ask whether the Zohar's reading of Jonah is an isolated phenomenon, or whether one can find signs or allusions to similar tendencies in the way the book of Jonah was understood during earlier centuries.

Two passages from chapter ten (printed edition) of *Pirke derabbi eli'ezer* come to mind in connection with this question. In one, Jonah, praying from inside the huge fish, says, "You are called *memit umeḥaye* [the One who brings death and who gives (or restores) life]. Behold, my soul has reached unto death; now restore me to life." In that same chapter of *Pirke derabbi eli'ezer*, Jonah, meeting Leviathan in the depths of the sea, informs the latter that "in the future I will descend and put a rope in your tongue [based on Job 40:25], and I will bring you up and prepare you [as a main dish] for the great feast of the righteous," an event slated to occur following the resurrection of the dead. The motif of Jonah's role in slaying Leviathan is introduced in connection with Jonah's promise to fulfill his vow (Jonah 2:10). In the context of the biblical story, that vow would be identified, instead, with his complying with the divine call to go to Nineveh. In a talmudic source (Avodah Zarah 3b),[23] the task of catching Leviathan for the great feast is assigned to the angel Gabriel, a task, it is mentioned, which the latter is unable to accomplish without divine help. In connecting that task instead with Jonah, the compiler of *Pirke derabbi eli'ezer* assigns to Jonah a role directly associated with the resurrection.[24] Scholem,[25] it is interesting to note, has identified *Pirke derabbi eli'ezer* as a major aggadic source for the Zohar.

Elsewhere (chapter 33), *Pirke derabbi eli'ezer* identifies Jonah with the son of the widow in Zarafat. That son—in the aggadic retelling of the episode in I Kings 17—dies and is restored to life through Elijah as a sign for all the generations "that there is a resurrection of the dead." In the biblical story, the widow's son becomes so ill that "he had no breath left in him" (I Kings 17:17); God hearkens to Elijah's prayer and "the spirit of the lad was restored to him and he lived" (I Kings 17:22). A single word in the biblical text suggests the midrashic identification with Jonah—the word *emet* (truth), which concludes the account in the biblical source ("And the woman said to Elijah, now I know that you are a man of God and the word of God in your mouth is truth." [I Kings 17:24]). As is explained in the Zohar, "For this reason he is called the son of Amittai (the name related to *emet*), as it is written here, 'and the word of God in your mouth is truth (*emet*)'" (2:197a).

The Islamic writer Mirkhond (Muḥammad Ibn Khavandshah Ibn Maḥmud)[26] also identifies the resurrected son of the widow with Jonah, as did Jerome in Christian tradition, along with various midrashic sources.[27] Traditions included in *Bereshit rabbah* 98:11 and *Midrash tehillim*, chapter 26,[28] also identify Jonah with the son of the widow from Zarafat, though without spelling out the same implications. The latter source mentions that Jonah was exempted from death and hence permitted to enter Paradise alive. It is interesting that a passage in *Tanna deve eliyahu, Seder eliyahu rabbah*, chapter 18,[29] identifies the son of that widow from Zarafat as the future Messiah-son-of-Joseph.[30] In different ways and via different paths, these comments from classical or medieval Jewish lore all link Jonah with the motif of resurrection. Might they, in turn, echo a still older tradition that reads the book of Jonah in the light of that concept?

It is interesting to note, in Islamic tradition, that in a hadith quoted by Birmidhi, Mohammed, in speaking of his own resurrection, declares, "If anyone says, "'I am greater than Jonah son of Amittai,' he is a liar."[31]

One possible reading of the linking of Jonah and resurrection might view it as the influence of the Christian reading of Jonah; Christian exegesis viewed Jonah as a prefiguration of the experience of death and resurrection attributed to Jesus. According to Matthew 12:40, and its explication of the idea of the "sign of Jonah" found elsewhere in the Gospels,[32] Jesus drew the analogy of his imminent death and resurrection with Jonah's deliverance from the fish, "for as Jonah was three days and three nights in the belly of the whale, so will the Son of Man be three days and three nights in the heart of the earth."[33] Some scholars regard this verse from Matthew as an interpolation;[34] but its very presence in the text of the Gospels may signal a widespread view of Jonah as a prefiguration of Jesus in early Christianity. The significance of Jonah in early Christian art, it has been pointed out,[35] is solely as a symbol of resurrection.

Louis Ginzberg[36] suggests the possibility that midrashic passages implying a messianic significance to Jonah may represent a Jewish adaptation of this Christian reading of Jonah. Without any explicit mention of Jonah, a passage in *Tanna deve eliyahu*, as we have noted, assigns a messianic role to the son of the Zarafat widow. Similarly, Jonah's eschatological role vis-à-vis Leviathan might be explained in terms of the same process, as might the statement in *Midrash tehillim,* chapter 26, that Jonah was exempt from experiencing death and allowed to enter into Paradise alive. Origen attacks the belief, found in a book of Celsum, the second-century anti-Christian pagan writer, that Jonah, rather than Jesus, be considered a divine figure.[37] The complex link between Jonah and resurrection might be explained in terms of that same impact of the Christian view of Jonah as a prototype of Jesus.

It is also possible, however, that the association of Jonah with resurrection predates Christianity. Erwin Goodenough[38] has pointed to various indications that together posit the possibility of an early Jewish tradition as a prototype of the Christian understanding of the fish and of Jonah as symbols of immortality (and resurrection), the associations that stand out in early Christian art. The Jewish motif of the Feast of Leviathan might reflect the actual practice, in various religious traditions, of a fish dinner as a foretaste of immortality. Other evidence for the fish as a Jewish symbol includes the fish figures in the art both of ancient synagogues and graves as well as various Jewish marriage customs, from widely dispersed geographic areas, in which the fish takes on the association of a fertility symbol, a significance psychologically akin to immortality.[39] One or two amulets showing Jonah together with the fish as signs promising immortality appear more likely to be of Jewish rather than of Christian origin.[40] Though lacking definitive proof, Goodenough has provided numerous examples of the fish as a sign of immortality in earlier strata of Jewish symbolism, suggesting the possibility that the link between Jonah and resurrection may have preceded the emergence of Christianity.

Goodenough[41] refers to the zoharic reading of Jonah as having essentially survived from a much earlier period. He also cites an earlier suggestion by Isador Scheftelowitz[42] that both Jesus' analogy of his imminent resurrection on the third day with Jonah's deliverance from the fish (Matthew 12:40) and the Gospel motif of Jesus' three days in the tomb draw precisely from such an ancient Jewish tradition of Jonah's death and revival, one that survived to surface many centuries later in the Zohar.[43]

We have noted various allusions within the midrashic tradition, and in *Pirke derabbi eli'ezer* in particular, which indicate an intimate link between Jonah and resurrection over an extended period of time. Contrary to the view that the Zohar's reading of Jonah represents a sudden surfacing of an ancient idea, these allusions locate the Zohar's reading of Jonah much more within the context of an ongoing tradition of interpretation. These same allusions may well reflect a more ancient tradition—whatever its precise source and historical motivation—that reread Jonah in terms of resurrection, echoing themes implicit in the biblical text itself and, much later, voiced clearly and unambiguously in the Zohar's retelling of the biblical story of Jonah.

Notes

This commentary on the Zohar's rendition of Jonah is an expansion and further development of my article, "The Zohar on Jonah: Radical Retelling or Tradition," which appeared in *Hebrew Studies* 31 (1990), 57-69. Material from that article is included here with permission of the editor of *Hebrew Studies*.

1. Another allegorical interpretation of Jonah, brought in connection with the dove (*yonah*) in the biblical account of the flood, is found in the *Ra'aya mehemna* (included in the Zohar text, 2:153b) and in *Tikkune zohar*, chapter 20, both comprising a later stratum of zoharic literature. There the contrast between the dove and the raven in the flood account might suggest a comparison between the teachers of Kabbalah and the much more affluent leadership of Spanish Jewry. See Baer, *History of the Jews in Christian Spain* 1:273-75.

2. Hayyim Schirmann, *Hashirah ha'ivrit besefarad uveprovans* 2:497.

3. Miriam Sugarman, *The Debate between the Body and Soul in Spanish Medieval Literature*.

4. Colbert I. Nepaulsingh, *Toward a History of Literary Composition in Medieval Spain*, 66.

5. Bahya ibn Asher, *Kad hakemah, kippurim*, 117b; the motif is also found elsewhere within the Zohar itself: 1:121a; 2:48a.

6. Note also, in this connection, Gershom Scholem, *Origins of the Kabbalah*, 404-05, 413, on the affinity of early Kabbalah with the philosophical accent on a spiritualization of Jewish belief despite Kabbalah's stance as a conservative force lending support for more normative rabbinic tradition. The Zohar (1:117a) explains that with resurrection, the soul will be joined not to a material body but rather to a body composed of light. See D. Cohen-Aloro, *Sod hamalbush umar'e hamal'akh besefer hazohar*, 59.

7. Ezekiel 37:1-14; *Yalkut shimoni* 2:375.

8. Baba Batra 16a.

9. James Frazer, *The Golden Bough*, 5-6; John Vickery, *Literary Impact*

of the Golden Bough, 54-55.

10. Otto Komlòs, "Jona Legends"; Hans Schmidt, *Jona*, 933-47.

11. William Simpson, *Jonah Legend*.

12. Eliade, *Myths, Dreams and Mysteries*, 219-33.

13. Maud Bodkin, *Archetypal Patterns in Poetry*, 79; Campbell, *Hero with a Thousand Faces*, 90-92, 207, 208, 251.

14. Simpson, *Jonah Legend*, 105.

15. Bodkin, *Archetypal Patterns*, 79.

16. Tabari (Abu Ja'far Muḥammad Ibn Jarir aṭ-Ṭabari), quoted in Komlòs, "Jonah Legends," 58; Al-Kisai, quoted in Komlòs, 61.

17. Mirkhond (Muḥammad ibn Khavandshah Ibn Maḥmud), as quoted in Simpson, *Jonah Legend*, 86. Note also Stefan Schreiner, "Muhammads Rezeption des Biblischen Jona-Erzëhlung" and the sources quoted in that study.

18. James Ackerman, "Satire and Symbolism in the Song of Jonah."

19. George M. Landes, "The 'Three Days and Three Nights' Motif' in Jonah 2:1" and "The Kerygma of the Book of Jonah."

20. Shalom Spiegel, *Last Trial*, 112 n. 182.

21. Ibid., 184.

22. See Megged, *Ha'or hanehshakh*, 120-21.

23. Also *Yalkut shimoni* 2:926 on Job 40.

24. The slaying of Leviathan for the eschatological feast might echo more ancient myths regarding the sea, sea animals, and spirits symbolizing the sea as a force for chaos threatening the order of creation. With the catching and slaying of Leviathan, creation is then secure from the threat of returning chaos. A passage included in the printed text of the Zohar (2:108b, *Sava de-mishpatim*) retells a talmudic legend about the pair of Leviathans not permitted to engender because of the grave danger posed to the world should their numbers increase.

25. Gershom Scholem, *Major Trends in Jewish Mysticism*, 170.

26. As quoted in Simpson, *Jonah Legend*, 85.

27. Louis Ginzberg, *Legends* 4:197.

28. *Midrash Tehillim*, ed. Solomon Buber, p. 220

29. *Tanna deve eliyahu, Seder eliyahu rabbah*, ed. Meir Friedmann, pp. 97-98.

30. Yehudah Leibes, in "Yonah ben amittai kemashiah ben yosef," has traced the sources that point to the identification of Jonah as Messiah the son of Joseph, an identification, as he points out, not found at all in the Zohar, but one that recurs in a seventeenth-century school of Polish Lurianic Kabbalah.

31. David Halperin, *The Faces of the Chariot: Early Jewish Responses to Ezekiel's Vision*, 486; I am indebted to the author for pointing out this reference to me.

32. Luke 11:29-32; note also Mark 8:11.

33. Drawing upon the Septuagint's translation of Jonah 2:1.

34. Kristen Stendahl, *The School of St. Matthew*, 132-33; Green, *Gospel According to Matthew*, 128-29.

35. Robert Hood Bowers, *Legend of Jonah*, 20-29.

36. Ginzberg, *Legends* 6:351 n. 38.

37. Origen, *Contra Celsum* 7:57, included in *Patrologia Graeca*, 824; trans. Chadwick, 442-43; cited also in Friedlander's translation of *Pirke derabbi eli'ezer*, 73 n. 1.

38. Erwin Goodenough, *Jewish Symbols in the Greco-Roman Period.*

39. Ibid. 5:47-53; 12:96, 101.

40. Ibid., 5:48.

41. Ibid., 5:47.

42. Isador Scheftelowitz, "*Der Fisch-Symbol in Judentum und Christentum*," 10-11.

43. Note also A. Jeremias, *Handbüch des altorientalischen Geisteskultur*, 167.

The Sefirah of Yesod, Foundation.

A Tale of Sin and Repentance

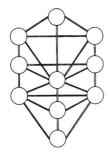

A mark on a man's face signifying a near-incestuous act is removed with his true repentance.

On route to Cappadocia[1] together with Rabbi Yose, Rabbi Abba noticed a man along the road with a particular mark that appeared as though engraved upon his face. Rabbi Abba suggested, "Let us turn from this road, for that face signifies that the person has transgressed the Torah's prohibition against incest[2] and that precisely for this reason he has that kind of mark on his face."

Rabbi Yose retorted, "Perhaps that mark was his already as a young child, and if so how could his be a case of incest?"

But Rabbi Abba insisted, "I perceive in his face a clear and certain sign that he has transgressed the biblical prohibition against incest." He then called to the man and said, "Tell me something. What is that mark upon your face?"

The man entreated, "Please, I request of you, do not add to my punishment, for my sins have brought this about." When Rabbi Abba went on to inquire as to the nature of his sins, the man told him, "One day my sister and I were traveling along the road. We took lodging at an inn where I indulged in wine in abundance and became intoxicated. And during that night I was holding my sister in an intimate and passionate embrace.[3] Then, when we rose in the morning, the innkeeper was quarreling with a man, and as I stood between them (in order to separate the two) I received blows from both sides. And while this consequent mark could have been fatal, I was saved only through the help of a physician who was present among us."

Rabbi Abba went on to inquire, "Who was the physician?"

The man answered, "Rabbi Simlai."

"What remedy did he give you?"

"Medicine for the soul. And from that very day I have engaged in repentance. Each day I see my face in a mirror and I cry before the Holy One, blessed be He, Master of the worlds, concerning that sin, and with those tears I wash my face."

Rabbi Abba remarked, "If it were not that the gravity of your sin precludes repentance, I would remove that scar from your face. But I nevertheless apply concerning you the verse, 'Your guilt shall depart and your sin be purged away'" (Isaiah 6:7).[4] Rabbi Abba told him to repeat that verse three times, and when he, in fact, uttered it three times the mark vanished. Rabbi Abba commented, "Certainly your Master wished to remove that mark from you as yours is beyond doubt a state of true repentance."

The man told Rabbi Abba, "I vow that from this day on I will devote myself day and night to the study of Torah."

Rabbi Abba then asked his name.

"Elazar," he answered.

Rabbi Abba commented, "*El azar* [God has helped]—certainly your name brought it about that God has helped you and has been your support," and Rabbi Abba sent him on his way with a blessing.

Sometime later, while on his way to visit Rabbi Simeon, Rabbi Abba came to the very town where this man lived and found him sitting and expounding Torah . . . . (Deliberating on the verse, "My gauntness serves as a witness and testifies against me" [Job 16:8], he explained that if one violates the laws of the Torah, the Torah itself then places a mark on that person's face which, furthermore, is bequeathed to children born while the parent is in that condition; if the child repents, however, then the evil legacy does not pass on to him, for "nothing stands in the way of repentance."[5] And in contrast, if a person lives a righteous life and studies Torah day and night, then the Holy One, blessed be He, weaves around him a thread of grace[6] and places upon him a mark that makes him secure in the face of all danger.)

Rabbi Abba said to him, "You have interpreted this verse beautifully. Where did you learn this interpretation?"

He answered, "So I have been taught. And I have similarly been taught that this evil spirit is then a legacy bequeathed to all one's children, unless they repent—as nothing stands in the way of repentance. And this I learned when that remedy was given to me at a time when I myself had such a mark engraved upon my face. For one day, while walking along the road, I met up with a righteous man, and through him that mark was removed from me."

Rabbi Abba asked him his name, and he answered, "Elazar." The sage then explained the man's name as *El azar* (God has helped), adding that He "has made you, as it were, another person."

Rabbi Abba continued, "Blessed is the Merciful One who brought it about that I have seen you and in particular that I am privileged to see you in your present state. Blessed is your portion in this world and in the World-to-Come." And he went on, "I am the one who chanced to meet you at that time." The man bowed down before Rabbi Abba and invited him to his house where he prepared for him three measures of bread and the meat of a three-year-old calf.[7]

After they had eaten, the man said, "Rabbi, tell me something. I have a red heifer,[8] the mother of the calf of whose meat we have now eaten. And one day, quite some time before she calved, as I was leading her to pasture to graze, a man passed before me and inquired of me as to the heifer's name. I told him that from the day of her birth I had never given her a name. The man declared, 'She will be called *Bat-sheva*, the mother of Solomon—should you merit atonement.' And when I turned around to see the man, he was gone. Afterward I thought this to be a silly thing. But now that I have learned some Torah I have been pondering his remark. Ever since the time that Rabbi Simlai left, there has been no one to enlighten us in matters of Torah as he had, and I hesitate to utter a word of Torah that I have not learned from a teacher; this remark I now recognize as a statement of secret wisdom, one, however, which I do not grasp."

Rabbi Abba said to him, "Certainly it is a mystery alluding to both the upper and lower worlds. In esoteric teaching a certain sefirah is actually called *Bat-sheva* (the daughter of seven)[9] [and is referred to as a red heifer]. And therefore all things (in Numbers 19) occur in groups of seven: seven cows, seven burnings, seven sprinklings, seven washings, seven times the term *tame* (impure, unclean), seven times the term *tahor* (clean, pure) and seven priests—including Moses and Aaron who are mentioned by name in the passage.[10] It is correct, as that man said who designated the name *Bat-sheva*, that it is entirely a mystery."

The man addressed Rabbi Abba, "Blessed be the Merciful One who enabled me to hear your words. Blessed be the One who, at the outset, greeted me [with peace], making possible what then happened to me, as it is written, 'Well (*shalom*, 'peace') with the far and the near—said the Lord [and I will heal them]" (Isaiah 57:19),[11] for by first extending peace to me when I was distant, the Holy One, blessed be He, brought me near to Him."

Rabbi Abba quoted concerning him the verse, "Greeting (*shalom*, 'peace') to you and to your household and to all that is yours!" (I Samuel 25:6)[12]

(3:75b-76b)

Notes

1. In Asia Minor. Elsewhere (2:38b), the Zohar refers to Cappadocia as a place where men of piety do not reside.

2. Leviticus 18:6-18.

3. The Aramaic word *ahidna* would signify "I held her" or "I held on to her," (see Scholem's note in *Sefer hazohar shel gershom scholem*, III, 75b). Though the use of the verb does not seem to indicate actual intercourse, the context of the story as a homily on the biblical prohibition of sibling incest imbues the brother's act as one with clear incestuous connotations.

4. The burning coals touching the lips of the prophet symbolize the removal of all sin and guilt on his part. Elsewhere (3:57b) the Zohar connects this verse with tears—appropriate to its use in our story. God is said to pronounce these words concerning the person who reads of the death of Aaron's sons (Leviticus 16) on Yom Kippur, lamenting and shedding tears. Note the commentary to the story that follows.

5. Hagigah 9a-b; Yebamot 22b.

6. "A thread of lovingkindness," Hagigah 12b. The term suggests the sefirah *hesed* ("lovingkindness"); while the Day of Atonement is usually identified with *Binah* as a divine archetype of repentance, a passage included in the printed text of the Zohar (2:135a) identifies it also with *hesed*.

7. A calf at a third of its full growth, or a calf in its third year, when it is tastiest, or the third calf of its mother (Eruvin 63a; Shabbat 11a; Sanhedrin 65b; also *Zohar hadash, No'ah* 22c).

8. The ashes of the red heifer (Numbers 19:2) were used to cleanse those ritually impure and restore them to a state of purity, enabling them to

participate in the cultic ritual of the Tabernacle and the Temple.

9. The Shekhinah (*Malkhut*, being the lowest of the seven lower *Sefirot*, hence derives from all those above). The Shekhinah, described as the "perfect red one" in terms of Her compassionate type of judgment, is symbolized by the red heifer. The symbolism is explained also in other ways: the ashes of the red heifer both purify the impure and render impure those who were previously in a state of cultic purity—in this case the officiating *kohen* (priest) and the person who carries out the ashes afterwards; this situation parallels the Shekhinah, with its connections with the higher world of Emanation and with the unholy forces of the *Sitra ahra* (Zohar 3:180b-181a; see Isaiah Tishby, *World of the Zohar*, 3:1166).

10. Comments in *Bamidbar rabbah* 19:2 and *Pesikta derav kahana, hahodesh*, 33a-b, note that in this passage, Numbers 19:1-22, seven things are mentioned, each of them seven times.

11. Midrashic sources interpret the "distant one" in this verse as the sinner who has repented (*Bamidbar rabbah* 11:7). In this vein, *Pesikta derav kahana* 44:8 presents a reading of this verse as "Peace, peace to the one who was distant but is now near," also in Zohar 2:21a. A passage in *Bamidbar rabbah* 44:8, noting that mention of peace to the distant one precedes the greeting of peace to him that is near, explains, on the basis of this verse, that God extends peace to the distant one even sooner than to him that is near. Sanhedrin 99a includes the comment, on the basis of this same verse, that even the completely righteous person, without sin or flaw, cannot attain the level occupied by the former sinner who has repented.

Mention of peace in the verse is preceded by the clause, "I create the fruit of the lips." As in Isaiah 6:7, the association of repentance with speech assumes significance in this story in which Elazar's words of Torah and his devotion to a life of studying the words of Torah serve as a way of repentance and healing. The force of that association recalls the statement in Berakhot 34b in which God's healing a person depends upon the strength—or fluency—of "the fruit of his lips."

12. Words David instructed his young men to relay to Naval and Abigail.

Commentary

The above story, together with the discourse of Elazar, the penitent, within the frame of the story, comprises the Zohar's homily on Leviticus 18:9, "The nakedness of your sister—your father's daughter or your mother's, whether born into the household or outside—do not uncover their nakedness." And yet the reader will note that the discourse of Elazar, located within the frame of this story, nowhere explicitly relates to or even mentions this verse. The subject of Elazar's discourse—at least on the surface—is not incest but rather repentance (*teshuvah*), and the story containing it is a tale of sin and repentance.

On a more subtle level the reader locates a connection between the homily and the verse it interprets, a connection revolving around the verb *glh* (uncover). This verb is part of the term for incest, *gilui arayot* ("uncovering of nakedness"—of the most intimate parts of the body), and the meaning of the verb echoes in the story in that the mark uncovers and discloses a person's hidden sin. Incest is, by nature, an act concealed from public attention; in the story this hidden act is revealed, uncovered, by means of a visible mark on Elazar's face. Later in the story, the hidden meaning of the enigmatic utterance concerning the name of the heifer is similarly "uncovered" and deciphered.

Several other threads interconnect in the story to contribute to an intricate structure and narrative art. The names of both the penitent and the heifer have significance, and the importance of the name in each case reinforces that of the other. The tale is, in part, a story of recognition as Rabbi Abba, hearing the name Elazar—a name he himself had interpreted—recognizes that the man expounding Torah is the same person whom he had healed at an earlier point in time. The note, voiced at the story's conclusion, of drawing the distant one near echoes the beginning of the tale where Rabbi Abba, rather than turning aside from the road as he was about to do, instead calls to the stranger and speaks with him. The story goes beyond the analogy of *teshuvah*, a true turning away from sin, and physical healing, to an actual identification of repentance with physical healing: with repentance the mark is removed from the sinner's face. And the mention of the red heifer toward the end of the story recalls the biblical law and practice of the use of the ashes of that heifer in connection with purifying the ritually impure, a rite that symbolically parallels the sinner's repentance following his initial immoral act.

The penitent who is seen teaching a message of repentance is himself a living proof text of his teaching. The precise details of that teaching include an especially jarring note: the impure spirit of the sinner, we hear, is inherited by children born of spiritually impure parents. The child thus bears the guilt of his parents' sin, a sin for which the child is in no way responsible and is unjustly victimized. The injustice in such cross-generational sin and punishment, however, is countered precisely by the power of repentance that prevails over the inherited impurity; repentance offers the child the possibility to free himself of those ill effects, and a thread of grace then supplants the mark of sin.

As a tale of repentance, the story develops through stages in the confirmation of penitence, stations along the path to complete atonement. First comes the stage of healing, accomplished through the assistance of Rabbi Simlai, who guides the sinner in the path of recovery through repentance. Later, Rabbi Abba's willingness, despite his initial hesitation, to effect the scab's disappearance, reaffirms the genuineness of the man's repentance. As another step, the sinner fulfills his vow to study Torah day and night as his way of penance. Finally, an explanation is offered to an enigmatic and seemingly meaningless utterance, an explanation which, in context, confirms the fact of Elazar's repentance and pronounces atonement for his past iniquity.

Though effected by human agents, all these steps in repentance and in its confirmation are essentially divine acts, as suggested by the very name *Elazar* (God has helped). The internal logic of the story precludes their being interpreted as chance occurrences. Following his enigmatic utterance concerning the heifer, the speaker disappears, signaling divine involvement in his bizarre meeting with Elazar. The verse from Isaiah quoted toward the very end of the story ("Well with the far and the near—said the Lord—[and I will heal them]") serves as a clinching proof text that it is God—even when acting through human agents—who calls to the sinner and leads him to the road of repentance. In light of this verse, the narrative acquires an additional dimension, and even while Rabbi Simlai and Rabbi Abba are human guides to repentance, God is seen as the Master of Repentance behind the scene.

The story is constructed also upon a series of antitheses all pointing to the basic polarity of sin and repentance. The sin takes place at an inn where Elazar's intoxication paves the way for his near-incestuous act, and where quarreling results in the blows that directly pro-

duce the sign of sin. The antithesis—and rectification—of the inn setting, with its intoxication and contention, is found in the meal to
which the penitent invites Rabbi Abba. The earlier overabundant
consumption of wine followed by the sinful act contrasts with an
occasion of eating accompanied by Torah. The study of Torah serves
as the very antithesis of sin, and unlike the quarreling at the inn, the
later meal accompanied by words of Torah concludes with an accentuated note of peace ("Greeting [*shalom*] to you and to your household and to all that is yours,") the *shalom* that is both the sign and
consequence of repentance.

Torah study aimed at developing self-control—a person's mastery
over his deeds and his passions—contrasts sharply with the young
man's state at the inn, in which he abandons himself to unconscious
impulse. Wine is mentioned elsewhere in the Zohar as symbolizing
the forces of strict judgment within the configuration of the *Sefirot*
and is associated with chaos and evil (1:73a-b); such moral chaos
stands in direct polarity with a life lived according to Torah.

Within this tale of a sinner's repentance no mention whatsoever is
made of the effect of the episode upon the penitent's sister. Her
whereabouts are not even mentioned, and in this regard the story
definitely fails our contemporary sensibilities.

When one contemplates the story as a whole from a distance, a
larger underlying pattern begins to emerge. The narrative crosses
back and forth over the line separating the visible from the concealed.
Physical manifestations are both effected by and affect events in the
moral-spiritual realm. A spiritual "remedy" removes a visible physical
mark, just as a secret sin brings on that mark which, in turn, is
responsible for leading the sinner to repentance. And the tears flowing from Elazar's inner state of remorse and repentance contribute to
healing the scab upon his face. Sin and repentance constitute the subtle unseen connections in the story; both the mark and its removal
serve only as external consequences of sin and repentance, respectively. The essential causes of happenings in the visible world are located
on a plane beyond that of physical appearances.

Similarly, an esoteric truth clarifies and uncovers the hidden
meaning of the enigmatic utterance relating to the heifer's name; a
detail of the complex symbolism relating to what is beyond the visible
hence provides the crucial link affirming, once and for all, the sinner's

repentance and atonement. What is on the surface a tale of sin and repentance alludes on a deeper level to the ultimate significance of mystic truth. A story voicing a conventional theme in the corpus of moral tales also alludes to a distinct ideology.

———————————————————————

Proceeding beyond the narrative art evident within the text and its structure, we might note a few biblical sources the story recalls. The mark on the sinner's face recalls the biblical "mark of Cain" (Genesis 4:15), even though it has a decidedly different role. In the zoharic tale, it is a mark of sin itself, rather than a means of protection for one who has transgressed. As conveyed in Elazar's discourse within the story, such a mark of disgrace signaling the presence of sin can, through repentance, be replaced with a sign having the very opposite effect, becoming one that like the biblical "mark of Cain" protects the bearer from danger.

The story also recalls the biblical episode in which the daughters of Lot, believing themselves and their father to be the world's sole survivors, plot to conceive children by him (Genesis 19:31-35), and it repeats that episode's association of intoxication with incest. That association is spelled out more emphatically in a talmudic statement, "Wine leads to unchastity" (Nazir 4b). Comments upon the episode of Lot and his daughters included in *Bereshit rabbah* 51:8 stress that on the first night, when he has intercourse with his older daughter, Lot is totally unaware of what was happening due to the intoxicating effect of the wine he has consumed; only upon awakening in the morning does he know what has transpired. The same note is found in Nazir 23a, which adds, however, that knowing this, Lot nevertheless goes on to drink wine again the following night, prior to the act of intercourse with his younger daughter.

In various strands of the story, echoes of various motifs and episodes in midrashic sources produce a more subtle intertextuality. The name Elazar brings to mind the biblical figure Eliezer, the servant of Abraham, who, while his master was still childless, was said to rule over all that belonged to Abraham. According to a comment in *Bereshit rabbah* 59:8,[1] these words indicate that, like his master Abraham, the servant, too, prevailed over his evil inclination (*yetser hara*), the latter term often implying sexual drive. And the biblical motif of the mark of Cain recalls the aggadic motif that Cain afterward repented *[Bereshit rabbah* 22:13], a motif further emphasized in a midrashic comment, "He [God] made him [Cain] a sign for repentants" (Ibid., 12:12). Logical difficulties in the biblical account of the very first generations evoked the idea that both Cain and Abel were born with twin sisters intended as their wives (*Bereshit rabbah* 22:2-3; *Pirke derabbi eli'ezer*, chapter 21). In the latter source, and also in Sanhedrin 58b, we find a theme later developed in kabbalistic writings prior to the Zohar: even though intercourse with one's sister is clearly prohibited in the Torah, during the very first generation(s) it was permitted as an act of divine lovingkindness (*ḥesed*), there being no other women in the world for the sons of the first generations to take as wives.[2] Echoes of all these strands from earlier Jewish lore are heard in the story.

───

In this narrative the reader notes with remarkable clarity the complex relation of the zoharic story to its textual context. The greater portion of the Zohar's homilies on the Torah portion *Aḥare mot*, preceding this story, relate to the Toraitic account of Yom Kippur found in Leviticus 16. The themes of atonement, purification, and tears as a means of atonement are all present in the exegesis in these homilies. We find here an elaboration of the cultic function of the High Priest on Yom Kippur when he alone makes the pronouncement, *titharu* (You shall be purified.) (3:67a). The Zohar text includes an explanation of the Torah reading on Yom Kippur, which opens with mention of the death of Aaron's two sons. This portion is read, we are told, so that the listeners may experience grief, for when one grieves and sheds tears for the righteous who have died, God then forgives those who so grieve and addresses them, "Your guilt shall depart and your sin be purged away" (Isaiah 6:7). This same biblical verse is heard in the story in connection with the removal of the mark of sin upon the penitent's face.

While the story comprises a homily on a verse from a later passage from that Torah portion, one not relating to Yom Kippur, the themes associated with Yom Kippur are nevertheless distinctly present in the narrative. With repentance, the sinner attains atonement, and his tears, with which he washes his face, are crucial to the disappearance of the mark of sin. The mention of the red heifer in the story also recalls the biblical rite of purification (Numbers 19) which parallels the rite of Yom Kippur (Leviticus 16).

An additional theme that recurs in these same homilies preceding our story is the value of Torah, including Torah spoken during the course of a meal. Those homilies tell of sages who rise at the midnight hour to study Torah (3:67b). Earlier, the text relates an episode in which a group of sages are eating together and Rabbi Simeon bar Yohai suggests that each of them offer a new thought relating to the Torah (3:60b). In addition, the zoharic author states that the only sounds heard above in the higher realms of being are the voices of those engaged in Torah study (3:61a). It is also written that the highest kind of union to which one can aspire, namely union with the Holy Name, is effected precisely by accomplishment in Torah study (3:61a). The context of Yom Kippur and the atonement theme has the effect of assigning to Torah study a key role in the process of atonement. Though the biblical source in Leviticus, in its description of the ritual atonement, makes no mention of the study of Torah, the zoharic author, interpreting that biblical source, makes the point that Torah study enables the person remote from God to come near to Him, so that he is given the greeting of *shalom* (3:64a-b). This statement conveys most explicitly that Torah study is a means of atonement; it also foreshadows the conclusion of our story. The penitent, in the tale, expresses his repentance through a devotion to the study of Torah; his commitment to Torah study signifies the new person he has become in his path toward atonement following his unconscious sinful activity. The full measure of atonement is granted to the former sinner who has become a student of Torah.

Shortly before the story appears in the Zohar text, the subject of incest is discussed in a way that lends an additional dimension to the near-incestuous act in the story. It is explained that when the sons do not fulfill the will of the King—when the people of Israel do not fulfill God's Will—the King separates from the Shekhinah who is then kept at a distance from the King's palace, a situation equivalent to an incestuous state within the higher realms (3:74b). An incestuous act, it is here implied, ultimately symbolizes sin itself, all acts in which

Israel fails to fulfill the Divine Will. The separation within the higher realms effected by sin is itself a kind of ultimate nakedness, an incestuous condition.[3] This discourse provides a much vaster symbolic significance to the story which then appears shortly afterward in the text of the Zohar.

Somewhat earlier in the zoharic homilies on *Aḥare mot,* it is written that with the joy of union that the King and the Shekhinah experience, the palace officials also rejoice and are forgiven for all the sins through which they offended the King (3:66a). An incestuous condition in the higher realms, it is implied, would negate that very possibility of forgiveness.

The theme of incest together with those of tears, purification, atonement, and Torah study, all interwoven within the Zohar's dialectic discourse, go on to reverberate in the story as overtones of those themes already sounded in the text. Furthermore, they present a distinct antithesis between incest and Torah study in terms of their impact upon the higher worlds: human incest symbolizes a higher state of incest, of separation and nakedness within the divine realm, whereas Torah study effects union within the divine.

Apart from its role as a homily on a biblical verse prohibiting incest, the story could actually have dealt with any other grave sin without marring either the narrative or the homiletical teaching located within the text. On the surface, in other words, the theme of incest would not appear crucial to the narrative per se. However, as evident even more clearly in the text following the story, the literal and symbolic meanings of incest merge: prohibited acts of sexual union effect separation within the higher realms of being and "uncover higher nakednesses," having a detrimental effect upon the Shekhinah and hence also effecting separation between the letters of the Ineffable Name of God (3:77b-78a).

At the same time, the text points out—as does the teaching of the penitent within the story—that "nothing stands in the way of repentance, especially if the sinner accepts his punishment, as David did" (3:78b). This latter note contributes an additional nuance: the figure of the penitent sinner in the story is, by implication, assimilated to the figure of the biblical king in both his sin and his repentance.

An act interpreted as incestuous behavior in the zoharic story invites comparison with the medieval Christian legend of Pope Gregory.[4] Himself the son of an incestuous union, abandoned by his mother and found and raised by a fisherman, Gregory goes on, unknowingly, to marry his mother. Later, realizing what he has done, he devotes years to penance, living as an ascetic and standing upon a rock on an isolated island for some seventeen years. When he is discovered, his devoutness so impresses the Church that he is chosen Pope, his election signaling the attainment of a long sought-after atonement.[5] The Gregorius legend is found in many variations and several European languages.[6]

The zoharic tale lacks most of the features of the Gregorius tale, a story-type that emerged in a medieval Christian Europe very likely under the influence of the highly deterministic Greek Oedipus legend, but which also included the nuances of Christian penance. Our zoharic tale also lacks many of the features found in a legend of Darab, included in the *Shah-nameh*, written by the early eleventh-century Persian poet Ferdowsi, a legend which does not include the mother-son incest found in the Gregorius tale.[7] Like the Gregorius legend, our story extends from an act of incest to complete repentance. Even allowing, however, for the severity of incest as one of three sins to be avoided under duress, if necessary even at the cost of one's life (Sanhedrin 74a), the austere and ascetic mood of the Gregorius legend is not present in the zoharic story. Elazar's penitence consists of a way of life that is valuable and positive in its own right, and the pursuit of Torah-study is compatible with a dinner setting at which an excellent calf is served!

The emphatically positive tone of this zoharic story also contrasts with the tone of much of Jewish pietism, and its prescriptions for repentance, as it emerged along the Rhineland during the twelfth and thirteenth centuries. It stands in contrast also with many tales of repentance found in kabbalistic ethical texts of the sixteenth and seventeenth centuries that speak of self-affliction as a way of penance.

Notes

1. Also *Midrash tanḥuma*, ed. Solomon Buber, 1:120.

2. Note Zohar 3:77a; Isaiah Tishby, *Mishnat hazohar* 2:623; Rashi on Leviticus 20:17.

3. In his *Book of the Pomegranate*, Moses de Leon spoke of matters relating to incest as deep and significant mysteries disclosed only by intimation (*The Book of the Pomegranate*, ed. Elliot Wolfson, 347-48). Moses de Leon explained the prohibitions of incest as related to the separations following from the state of absolute oneness during the course of emanation of the *Sefirot*, the forms of divine being and power in the Godhead, adding note of the prohibitions both to sever that state of oneness and to merge together that which is separated (348). As the fruit of the tree, man is not permitted to return to the root (350). Note also Tishby, *Mishnat hazohar* 2:621-23, and Efraim Gottlieb, *Hakabbalah bekitve rabbi bahya*, 75.

4. Stith Thompson, *Motif-Index of Folktales*, "Penance: Gregory on the Stone; Standing on a Stone Pillar as Penance for Incest, Q541.3"; also Antti Amatus Aarne, *Types of the Folktale* 933.

5. The tale is included in the *Gesta Romanurana*, a medieval collection of legends, written in Latin and translated to German only in the nineteenth century. The tale is included in Cholevius, 167ff. An outline of the legend is found in Otto Rank, *Incest Theme in Literature and Legend*, 285-86. For variations in various European literatures and parallel medieval Christian legends, see Rank, 271-99. While the *Gesta* is generally dated to the mid-fourteenth century, the legend can be seen to exist at least as early as the twelfth century. See Rank, 287.

6. A Jewish setting and adaptation of the Gregorious story, told as actual happenings related by the Ba'al Shem Tov, is found in Abraham Isaac Svivelman, *Sippure tsadikim hahadash* 9. Two studies have been written on this Eastern European Jewish version of the Gregorius tale: Gedeliah Nigal, "Concerning a Hasidic Manuscript from the Beginning of the Century," and Yoav Elstein, "The Gregorius Legend: Its Christian Versions and Its Metamorphosis in the Hasidic Tale." See also ASAI (Archives of the Jewish Folktale, Haifa University), #9996.

7. Ferdowsi (Abu ol-Qasem Mansur), "The Story of Darab," in , trans. R. Levy, 221-30.

The Sefirah of Malkhut, Kingdom; also Shekhinah, God's Feminine Aspect.

A Child's Tears and His Father's Resurrection

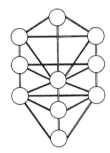

The impact of a young child's tears and words negate a decree of death and revive his dead father.

Rabbi Eleazar said, "Ḥaverim, let us go, in love and kindness, to a pomegranate[1] ripe and overflowing with juice whose name is Rabbi Yose of Peki'in.[2] For he has departed from this world without anyone coming to be with him and care for him, and he is nearby." They turned from the road and proceeded to go there. As soon as the townspeople caught sight of the guests, they all came out to greet them.

The *ḥaverim* entered the house of Rabbi Yose of Peki'in. The latter's young son allowed no one to approach the bed of his dead father; he himself was right next to him crying, his mouth cleaving to his father's mouth. The child was saying, "Master of the universe, it is written, 'If, along the road, you chance upon a bird's nest (in any tree or on the ground, with fledglings or eggs and the mother sitting over the fledglings or on the eggs, do not take the mother together with her young), let the mother go (and take only the young, in order that you may fare well and have a long life)'" (Deuteronomy 22:6-7).[3]

Weeping, he continued, "Master of the universe, fulfill this word written in Your own Torah. My younger sister and I are the two children of our father and mother. It was Your place to take us instead and to fulfill those words of the Torah; and do not object, Master of the World, that it is written 'mother' and not 'father,' for since our mother had died and was taken from her children, our father was as both father and mother to us. And now our father, too, who had been our protector, is taken from his children. Where is justice and the law of the Torah?" Rabbi Eleazar and the *ḥaverim* wept in hearing the lament and the crying of this child.

While Rabbi Eleazar began reciting the verse, "Like the heavens in their height, like the earth in its depth (is the mind of kings— unfathomable)" [Proverbs 25:3], a pillar of fire separated them, the child still cleaving to his father's mouth and not leaving him even for a single moment. Rabbi Eleazar declared, "Whether the Holy One, blessed be He, wishes to perform a miracle or whether He wishes that no one else (but the child) attend to him, the words and the tears of this child are too much for me."

While sitting, they heard a voice announcing, "Blessed are you, Rabbi Yose, for the words and the tears of this young child have ascended to the throne of the Holy King, and judgment has been given; God has designated for the Angel of Death thirteen persons in your place, and twenty-two years will be added to your life so that you might teach Torah to this child who is sincere and whole and beloved in God's eyes." Immediately they perceived that the fiery pillar had departed and Rabbi Yose opened his eyes, the mouth of his young son still cleaving to his mouth.

Rabbi Eleazar spoke, "Blessed is our lot in that with our very eyes we have seen the resurrection of the dead." They drew closer and the young son fell sound asleep as though he had expired from this world. The others said, "Privileged is your portion, Rabbi Yose, and beloved is the Merciful One who has brought a miracle to occur in response to the sobbing and weeping of your son; with his lovely words he has forced open a gateway to Heaven, and because of his young age years have been added to your life."

They took the child and kissed him and cried this time out of profuse joy. After they brought him out to another house he awoke, but they waited to inform him. Three days they rejoiced there, and together with Rabbi Yose they discovered many new ideas in the Torah.

Rabbi Yose then spoke to them. "*Haverim*, I am not permitted to reveal anything that I have seen in that other world until after twelve years will have passed. But the three hundred and sixty-five tears of my son ascended and were counted in the presence of the Holy King and, *haverim*, I can inform you that from the moment he began speaking, referring to that biblical verse (Deuteronomy 22:6-7) with tears breaking out with his words, three hundred thousand (righteous ones occupying) benches in the Academy on High all trembled and rose before the Holy King demanding compassion for me and offering themselves as a guarantee on my behalf.

"And the Holy One, blessed be He, was overcome with compassion for me, moved by those words and by the boy's willingness to offer his life for mine. One Guardian rose and said, 'Master of the World, behold it is written, "From the mouths of infants and sucklings (*yonkim*), You have founded strength on account of Your foes, to put an end to enemy and avenger" (Psalms 8:3). May it be pleasing to you to have pity on him by virtue of the Torah and by virtue of this youth who has expressed his willingness to offer his life for that of his father who was thus spared from death.' And He designated thirteen persons in my place and made a pledge sparing me from this severe judgment. In fairness, the Holy One, blessed be He, called to the Angel of Death, ordering him to return for me twenty-two years later.[4] For there is no alternative to His taking to Himself what He has lent to us. And now, *haverim*, as the Holy One, blessed be He, saw that you were truly worthy, He performed a miracle before your very eyes."

Rabbi Yose began expounding and said, "'The Lord deals death and gives life, casts down into *She'ol* and raises up' (I Samuel 2:6). One must examine this verse carefully, for does the Lord actually kill—His Name being the very elixir of life for all? Indeed, death cannot be attributed to Him, for everywhere His Name gives life to the whole world. What then is the meaning of those words, 'The Lord deals death'? The question is, how does He deal death? You might say that He brings on death through His departing from a person, for so long as He is with a person all the accusers in the world are unable to hurt him, though at the moment that He departs from a person, immediately the accusers all prevail over him and so he dies.

"That, however, is not the meaning. Rather, to whom does 'the Lord deal death'? He deals death to the impact of the evil Other Side.[5] Just as quickly as the impact of the Evil Side perceives the precious splendor of the Holy One, blessed be He, it immediately expires, vanishing from the world, and has no existence for even a single moment. God immediately resurrects. Whom does He resurrect? He restores to life the impact of the spirit of holiness that comes from the Side of Holiness and restores it to a state of complete being. All this the Holy One, blessed be He, accomplishes within the span of a single moment.

"And concerning what is written, 'He casts down into *She'ol* and raises up,' He brings that spirit of holiness down to the netherworld, immersing it there to cleanse it from sin and thereupon immediately brings it up to its proper place in the Garden of Eden. And as I departed from the world, *haverim*, my spirit also immediately departed from me, and I lay dormant until, a short while later, the Holy One, blessed be He, restored me to life—as my body had actually been dead. Just as soon as my son began to speak those words, his soul flew away and encountered my soul on its upward journey; in consequence of his purity and of the immersion it ascended to a place of judgment, and twenty-two years of life were given me because of my son's tears and words. And from this moment on, I must devote myself to what I had seen rather than to the things of the world. It is God's will that nothing that I had seen become forgotten and lost."

(Rabbi Yose went on to teach Torah, and his young son then added his own interpretation of a Torah passage. Amazed at his brilliant interpretation, his father embraced him, and the *haverim* wept and kissed him.)

The son said to him, "My masters, leave me with my father, for my spirit is still feeling faint." Rabbi Eleazar then inquired of Rabbi Yose, "How old is that child?"

"*Haverim*," he inquired, "I request of you not to ask, for he has not yet reached the age of five."

Rabbi Abba said, "I am astonished at the tender ones of this generation; what strength of mind they possess, like strong and lofty rocks!"

Rabbi Eleazar added, "Blessed is the lot of my father, the master of this generation, for behold in his days, the Holy One, blessed be He, willed to establish His two academies and to create for us a great and exulted academy as He desired. For there will not be a generation like this one until King Messiah will come."

(3:204b-206a)

Notes

1. A Jew full of *mitzvot* is likened to a pomegranate full of seeds (Berakhot 57a).

2. Peki'in is the village in the Upper Galilee where, according to Shabbat 33b and *Kohelet rabbah* 10:11, Rabbi Simeon bar Yohai together with his son Eleazar lived in a cave for thirteen years, hiding from the Romans.

3. Fledglings (*efroḥim*) can connote also very young children in school (Zohar 2:9a). Midrashic sources quoted this same verse as a principle of just behavior against which to measure the unjust events of history. Both *Eikhah rabbah* 1:37 (on Lamentations 1:9) and Pesikta derav kahana 78b include the comment that contrary to the law requiring the mother bird to be spared, the forces led by Sennacherib dashed mothers to pieces together with their children (Hosea 10:14). In *Bereshit rabbah* 76:5, and also in *Bereshit rabbati*, 147, Jacob, apprehensive about his meeting with Esau, feared the latter would smite both mother and children (Genesis 32:12), contrary to the law in Deuteronomy 22:6-7. See also *Bereshit rabbati*, 211. The use of the verse in this zoharic story echoes its use in those midrashic sources, and the same word pattern is used to voice the comparison.

4. Precedent in talmudic story (Baba Batra 11a). The number twenty-two connotes the twenty-two letters of the Hebrew alphabet and hence of the Torah that Rabbi Yose would teach his son.

5. *Sitra aḥra*, the demonic, unholy reality, which becomes powerful in the wake of human sin.

Commentary

This story is perhaps the most charming of all those found in the Zohar. Beyond this sheer charm, grasping the many allusions to other texts present in the story enhances our appreciation of the narrative.

Within this story, two biblical episodes resonate—even though the text nowhere explicitly refers to them. This phenomenon provides a significant yet subtle intertextuality to the story. The reader can recognize, in addition, strong similarities with another story from the Zohar itself. The traces of these stories imply comparisons with these narrative sources, and are keys to defining some of the more central themes of this story.

The *akedah* ("Binding of Isaac," Genesis 22), or more precisely the *akedah* as understood in the tradition of midrashic interpretation, echoes in several ways in the themes of this story.

Unlike the biblical source, some significant later midrashic interpretations read this episode in terms of Isaac's readiness to be bound on the altar, hence making Isaac rather than Abraham the real hero of the *akedah*. Samael (Satan), it is mentioned, seeks to dissuade Isaac from continuing along the journey to Moriah with his father; Isaac, however, continues walking with his father, even after learning that he will be the lamb for the offering (*Bereshit rabbah* 56:4). Isaac requests that his father bind his hands and feet lest he curse his father, showing him disrespect at the crucial moment (*Bereshit rabbah* 56:8; *Pirke derabbi eliezer*, chapter 31).[1] In our story, Rabbi Yose's son expresses not only a willingness but a definite request to die in place of his father. Precisely the purity and wholeness of intent in his wish to die that his father might live makes a powerful impression in the higher worlds.

Central to the story is the notion that the boy's readiness to die in place of his father is accepted in the higher realms with the result that his father's life is spared. According to a midrashic source, upon hearing the divine word not to harm his son in any way, Abraham feared that perhaps the sacrifice was somehow blemished and hence not acceptable; a heavenly voice then reassured him, "God has accepted your deeds" (*Vayikra rabbah* 20:2, quoting Ecclesiastes 9:7). Elsewhere in the Zohar (1:120ab), the command to sacrifice Isaac is said to have been executed and fulfilled on the level of spiritual intent. Such readiness, identified as the crucial element in the *akedah,* is fully present in this story in the pleading of the child.

The motif of tears, so significant in this narrative passage, recalls the theme of tears in various midrashic interpretations of the *akedah*. As Abraham took his knife, tears fell from his eyes into the eyes of his son (*Bereshit rabbah* 56:8). The angels, alarmed that Abraham might actually slaughter his son at the altar, cried aloud and wept (*Pirke derabbi eliezer*, chapter 31; also *Bereshit rabbah* 56:5, 7). In the latter source, angels' tears fell on Abraham's knife, blunting its sharpness and rendering it useless for striking his son. (Note also Zohar 1:120a for the motif of the angels' weeping at the Binding of Isaac.)

In describing the son's actual condition the story is vague, as though intentionally unclear. The reader might be led to ask: does the child who pleads to die in place of his father, in effect as a sacrifice, actually experience death in response to his request? We note that the boy's soul flew off to meet the soul of his father prior to the latter's return to life. Afterward, the child was found asleep "as one who is dead to this world." And at the end of the narrative, the son is still seen in a condition of fainting, a state suggesting the boundary between the presence and lack of consciousness—or between life and death. This ambiguity recalls the midrashic reading of the Binding of Isaac, where the actual death of Isaac upon the altar is followed by his resurrection to life. "When the sword touched his neck, Isaac's soul fled," only to return upon his hearing God's voice tell his father not to strike him. Isaac then praised God as One who "resurrects the dead" (*Pirke derabbi eli'ezer*, chapter 31).[2]

An entire cluster of themes found in the midrashic reading and re-creation of the Binding of Isaac echoes in the story of Rabbi Yose and his son; together they have the effect of depicting the boy as an Isaac-figure. The son in the story is a determined Isaac-figure who knows clearly what he is doing and toward what he is heading, and at the same time he is also a young and tender Isaac-figure likened in the text to a *gadya*, to a young goat or animal.

A more transparent biblical account also resonates in the story. The scene of the young son lying with his mouth upon the mouth of his dead father recalls the story of Elisha and the son of the Shunamite woman in II Kings, chapter 4:

Elisha came into the house, and there was the boy, laid out dead on his couch. He went in, shut the door behind the two of them, and prayed to the Lord. Then he mounted [the bed] and placed himself over the child. He put his mouth on its mouth, his eyes on its eyes, and his hands on its hands, as he bent over it. And the body of the child became warm. He stepped down, walked once up and down the room, then mounted and bent over him. Thereupon, the boy sneezed seven times, and the boy opened his eyes. (II Kings 4:32-35)

While the scene in the zoharic story clearly recalls the story of Elisha, the strength of the similarities subtly points to the difference between the redeeming or healing figures in the two accounts. Elisha was a *navi*, a prophet, and therefore in his case the reader's expectations are less jarred than in the case of the young child. In the zoharic story it is not a prophet but rather a child who annuls the fact of death; the comparison extols the child and places him on the same level as that of a prophet. The implied comparison brings to mind a statement found elsewhere in the Zohar: "Sometimes prophecy is placed in the mouths of children, and they prophecy even more that did the prophets in their time" (2:170a).

In addition to these two biblical narratives, a zoharic story with which we are already familiar, "Death Postponed" (1:217b-218b), echoes in this narrative. In both stories, imminent death threatening a sage is averted, and the spiritual power of a living human person is able to prevail over death. In both, the sage standing on the threshold of death has a young child, and the responsibility of teaching that child is a significant factor in the commutation of the death decree. The significant similarities between the two stories suggest that this story is actually a kind of revision of the earlier story, that the author, in his imagination, continued to relive and to give new form to the same basic scenario.

The author, if I am correct, reworked the same themes and motifs, creating, in the process, a distinctly different narrative. Whereas in the earlier story, imminent death is averted, this second story opens with the more radical situation in which death has actually occurred, and the narrative's dramatic dimension is hence significantly heightened. Another difference, equally obvious, is the hero-figure who saves the sage from death or who revives him. In "Death Postponed," the hero is none other than Rabbi Simeon bar Yohai, the mystic-sage par excellence in the Zohar. In this second story, in contrast, it is a young child, the sage's son who has died. A child, it is implied, is placed on a level with the greatest of the mystics and sages.

As in previous stories we have examined, various themes and motifs from the zoharic exegesis preceding the story go on to reverberate in the narrative text. Together they echo in the story and create a thematic matrix within which to grasp the story's meanings.

In the homilies prior to the story, zoharic exegesis on the Torah portion *Balak*, the following are among the notes seen later to be of significance in connection with the story: a description of judgment, following death, in the heavenly academy (3:185b), and the statement that death, together with the *Sitra aḥra*, held no power over the Israelites before the latter sinned by making the Golden Calf

(3:193a). And we read, in addition, of young children innocent of the taste of sin (3:198a).

Closer still to the story in the text of the Zohar is an interesting account of the Accuser (Satan) who, on Yom Kippur, attributes the fasting of the Israelites to their sins and wrongdoings but cannot comprehend why their innocent and pure children are also fasting. When told that despite their innocence they are nevertheless given over to the Accuser's servant and assistant, the Accuser himself, in pity, pleads before God to save those children from death and, furthermore, rescues them himself from the hands of his underling (3:202b-203a).

Additional notes reverberating later in the story include mention of the prayer of the poor, which, coming from one who is brokenhearted, cleaves all the windows of the firmament and takes precedence over all other prayers (3:195a); the parallel with the prayer of Rabbi Yose's son is obvious. And David is mentioned as one of those ready to sacrifice themselves in martyrdom (3:195a-b), a motif that echoes in the orphan son's willingness to sacrifice his own life in order to restore life to his father. An additional note of significance for the story is the account of a person whom thieves are planning to attack along the road; he is spared, however, when another person appears and becomes victim of the robber gang. The same motif of substitution, we recall, is present in the story first as Rabbi Yose is himself designates a substitute for a namesake of his, and later when thirteen persons altogether are given over into the hands of death as his substitute.

After likening the Torah, with its several layers of meaning, to the makeup of a tree, the author explains the Toraitic prohibition of destroying trees during a wartime siege (Deuteronomy 20:19) as a warning addressed to the forces of judgment to spare the devout student of Torah, the town's scholar who is himself a "tree of life." Since the destruction of the Temple, we are told, only in the learning of such a person does the Shekhinah find benefit, pleasure and even sustenance (3:202a-b). In our story, which follows shortly afterward in the text, the forces of judgment, responsible for the father's death, were defied, and a "tree of life" was spared.

Death and the limits of its power, the innocence of children and the wonder child, pleading to spare the innocent, the powerful prayer of the broken-hearted, the willingness to die, substitution, and the sparing of a scholar in judgment—all these go on to echo in a single narrative that follows.

In a broader sense, the story connects with the Zohar as a whole—the father's restoration to life echoes the theme of the conquest of death in the Zohar. Like "Death Postponed," it alludes to a future Redemption when God will annihilate death itself; the forces of holiness will then prevail decisively over those of evil, which contain the roots of death. Since in the zoharic view of reality death lacks intrinsic or permanent being and power, the author's narrative imagination could limit and defer it and, within limits, even annul the fact of a death that has occurred. The belief in the ultimate conquest of death is voiced explicitly in the homiletical passage located within the story. And somewhat further on, the very conclusion of the zoharic exegesis on Balak includes an apocalyptic scenario of future events. There the author states that God "will raise the dead from among his people and they will forget death" (3:212b). Just as many notes from the previous pages of the Zohar text echo in the story, the story itself, via the theme of resurrection, reverberates in the statement at the end of the Zohar's homilies on that Torah portion. We note here again an example of a story relating events occupying an extremely limited time span, one that nevertheless reflects an infinitely broader story encompassing all of cosmic history.

By virtue of his tears and his words, the story relates, the son makes an emphatic impression upon God and upon the forces on high.

His tears are able to break the barriers and to ascend to the very throne of God, the distant throne surrounded and protected by impenetrable gates and impediments. The reader's response to those same tears parallels that of God and the heavenly judges.

The place of tears in this story reflects the thematics of tears in the Zohar as a whole. We are told in the name of Rabbi Judah, "Man's destiny depends ultimately upon repentance and prayer, and above all upon prayer with tears, for there is no gate that tears are unable to penetrate" (2:12b). The Zohar goes on to stress that both

Israel's exile and redemption depend solely upon weeping, upon the tears of Esau and Rachel, respectively (2:12b). In expanding upon a talmudic motif (Berakhot 59a), the zoharic author informs the reader that each day at dusk as God recalls His young children's distress, two divine tears fall into the sea (2:9a).

The child's words, directed to God, voice his willingness to die as a substitute for his father. At the opening of the story, it is related that Rabbi Yose of Peki'in was himself designated to die as a substitute for a namesake of his (according to Cordovero's commentary, *Or hayakar,* Rabbi Yose ben Lakonia, Rabbi Eleazar's father-in-law) who is dying.[3] And later in the story, we note that in place of the boy's father, Rabbi Yose of Peki'in—obviously an exceptional person—the Angel of Death is given thirteen people as a substitution. (People were not always considered to be of equal value!) A substitution is required to provide compensation to the Angel of Death (note Zohar 1:174b). These two examples of involuntary substitutions mentioned in the story direct the reader's thoughts to the case of the child who voluntarily and willingly asks to die so that his father might live, a request voiced in the child's words.

The boy's words connect with his interpretation of a Torah passage concerning Zelafhad, the father who dies leaving five daughters and no sons (Numbers 27). According to the child's interpretation of that passage, Zelafhad dies because of words he had uttered—he had not been careful in his speech before Moses. He dies in the wilderness (*midbar*), suggesting the root *dbr* (speak). Through an integration of the narrative and the homiletic content of the same passage, the reader, like the child himself (3:205b), comes to grasp that the spoken word is capable both of causing death and of restoring life.

The emphasis upon the spoken word also connects with a leitmotif of the "mouth" present in the zoharic homilies on this Torah portion. It is mentioned that *pi ha'eton* (the mouth of Bilaam's animal, Numbers 22), the mouth of the earth that swallowed Korah and his followers (Numbers 16), and the mouth of the Well of Miriam, sister of Moses,[4] were all created at the moment of twilight immediately before the sabbath of creation (quoting the concept found in Mishnah Avot 5:9). In contrast, "the mouth of the Lord" came into being within the time span of the seventh day as God hallowed that day (3:201a). Shortly afterward in the text of the Zohar, Rabbi

Pinḥas, upon coming to Rabbi Simeon bar Yohai, uttered the words, "I kiss the mouth of the Lord" (3:201b), a way of praising the mouth that has spoken brilliant teaching. The power of the wicked Bilaam, it is later reported (3:206b) was in his mouth. The utterances of Bilaam and those of the young boy in the story are obviously antithetical in character. Bilaam's knowledge, furthermore, belongs to the night hour (3:206b), whereas the opportune moment of prayer, specifically a prayer for healing, is at the hour of dawn, the hour of lovingkindness, for it is then that the angel Raphael goes forth with medications for the purpose of healing (3:204a). The antithetical nature of the two kinds of speech illumines the child's words of pleading and connects with the child's act of placing his mouth over his father's in his effort to revive him.

Significantly, the author interweaves into the story the following verse: "From the *mouths* of infants and sucklings/You have founded strength on account of Your foes, to put an end to enemy and avenger" (Psalms 8:3, italics mine). This verse, as quoted in the story, refers directly to the boy's pleading words, but the reader detects that they relate, in addition, to his impressive homiletical interpretations of the Torah.

In his pleading, the son quotes from Deuteronomy 22:6 concerning the sending away of the mother bird. And while that verse is utilized in midrashic sources for a similar purpose of measuring real events with a yardstick of justice and compassion, in our story the author, it would seem, is attracted to the word *efroḥim* ("fledglings") in the same verse; in the context of the story, that word alludes to the child himself and accentuates the pathetic situation of orphan children.

In the introduction, I discussed the role of biblical verses within the zoharic narratives. I noted there that even when the plain meaning of a quoted verse relates in a meaningful way to the story, the verse at times also evokes associations based upon rabbinical sources, creating a network of overtones. As an example, the verse from Psalms quoted above connotes interpretations of the verse found in midrashic texts. This verse is associated with the motif of the Israelites' receiving the Torah only after they had offered their children as surety to God (*Shir hashirim rabbah* 1:4; *Bamidbar rabbah* 9:7). The same verse is also associated with the motif of "infants and sucklings," after the crossing of the Reed Sea, opening their mouths to join in the song of praise sung by Moses and the Israelites (*Mekhilta derabbi yishma'el, Deshirata,* chapter 1).[5] In *Bamidbar rabbah* 9:7 it is said, on the basis of this verse, that young children comprise God's sole majesty in the world.

The choice of a particular biblical verse, like the implied but subtle comparison with biblical episodes and their aggadic interpretations and with another zoharic story, stresses the centrality of the child figure in this narrative.

As in "Death Postponed," the figure of the child connotes renewal, hope, and continuity. The archetypal association of the child with innocence lends still another dimension to the child's role as the redeeming figure in the story: as death has an association with the sin of Adam and with sin itself, the child in his very nature suggests a world of purity and wholeness preceding the introduction of death into the world. The child figure is a kind of personification of Eden, a condition lacking blemish, defilement, or moral complexity. To the zoharic author and his particular spiritual milieu, the word "sucklings," *yonkim,* in Psalms 8:3, suggested an association with the concept of the *yanuka,* the wonder child capable of offering brilliant interpretations of Torah.

Following the wisdom heard from the mouth of this child, not yet five years old, the text of the Zohar goes on to mention the wondrous level of the tender children of that generation. It speaks in effect of a collective *yanuka;* the child-archetype has shifted from a single child to an entire generation of such wonder children.

The motif of the wonder child was part of the cultural landscape of medieval Spain. It is related, for example, that King Alfonso X, at the age of two, was able to chant the Ave Maria; when he was just old enough to read he was taken to St. Eugenio, who described him as the best student he had ever taught.[6] Joseph Jones[7] has traced the wondrous child motif in Spanish literature to rabbinical legends concerning Abraham that entered the general stream of Spanish literature during the thirteenth century.[8] Abraham's legendary youth and his conversion to true belief as a young boy served as the model of the self-trained philosopher in Spanish writing and lore of the time.

Abraham's mother, that tradition claimed, found her baby absorbed in pious studies in the cave where he was placed in hiding. Also Alexander, while still a child, was portrayed in Castilian poetry as having surpassed his masters in the skills of intellectual argument.[9]

The zoharic author's fascination with the figure of the *yanuka*, however, appears to go beyond its parallels in medieval Spanish writing. For the Zohar, we might venture, this figure suggests a certain childlike and intuitive mind, one fully open, without inhibition, to the world of imagination.

The type of knowledge most valued in the spiritual world of the Zohar is not that possessed by those who have necessarily studied in a disciplined way over the course of many years, as would be the case with either *halakhah* (Jewish law) or philosophy. It is rather the fruits of a fresh mind, one capable of sudden insight, which is grasped as a disclosure of the deeper meaning of the Torah. Insight of this nature can emerge in the inspiration of the moment. It need not fit into a comprehensive pattern of thinking but can be fragmentary and even abound in self-contradiction. Though the Zohar also includes examples of the figure of the elderly man as bearer of wisdom, ultimately it is not the elder scholar who most precisely personifies the Zohar's mindset, but rather the child with a fresh mind, open to wonder and enchantment, the child who is master of brilliant insights. The Zohar has an affinity to "childlike" qualities and to a tenderness of mind in which the analytical does not subdue the intuitive. Its spirit is more accessible to the imagination than to the disciplined mind and is expressed in the qualities of the mythopoetic creativity.[10]

In stories such as the one under discussion, the author of the Zohar, whether consciously or unconsciously, paints in the figure of the brilliant wonder child a mirror-image of his own temperament. The *yanuka* symbolizes the richness of imagination and of the intuitive which pervades the Zohar.*

Notes

This commentary is an expansion and further development of a lecture included in the *Proceedings of the Tenth World Congress of Jewish Studies*, Division C, Volume 1 (Jewish Thought and Literature, Hebrew section), Jerusalem, 1990, 333-37. Material from this paper, presented at the 1989

World Congress of Jewish Studies, is included here with the permission of the World Union of Jewish Studies, Jerusalem.

1. Note also the commentary of Bahya ben Asher on Genesis 22:7.

2. For numerous parallels throughout the midrashic sources, see Shalom Spiegel, *Last Trial*, 28-59.

3. 'In the same commentary, Cordovero explained Proverbs 25:3 as the inability to grasp the logic or justice in such exchange or substitution.

4. Aggadic motif of the well of fresh water that accompanied the Israelites in the desert only to dry up upon Miriam's death. *Ta'anit* 9a; *Bamidbar rabbah* 1:2, 14:20; Tosefta Sotah 11:10.

5. Also *Yitro, baḥodesh*, chapter 3 in the same midrashic source, Sotah 30b, and *Mekhilta derashbi* on Exodus 19:17.

6. Quoted from the *Vida de San Ildefonso*, in John Esten Keller, *Pious Brief Narrative*, 74.

7. Joseph Jones, "From Abraham to Andrenio."

8. Ibid., 70-73.

9. Harriet Goldberg, "Literary Portrait of the Child," especially 20 nn. 24, 50, 62.

10. Daniel Matt, *Zohar*, 26, contrasts the Zohar in this respect with the Hebrew, nonpseudepigraphic writings of Moses de Leon.

About the Papercut Art:
The Ten Sefirot

Diane Palley

The Jewish mystical tradition of the Kabbalah teaches that there are ten *Sefirot* or levels that occur between the world as we know it and the God whom we can never know. The concept of the "emanations of God" has been developed over the centuries into a rich and complex system of associations, drawing from the Bible, nature, and human experience. Within this system, each *sefirah* is connected to elements in many different categories.

The first three *Sefirot*—*Keter, Hokhmah,* and *Binah*—form a triad that stands apart from and above the lower seven. These "intellectual" *Sefirot* contain fewer of the images and associations, such as biblical personalities, days of creation, and aspects of nature, than the other *Sefirot.* The second triad consists of *Hesed, Din,* and *Tiferet,* considered the *Sefirot* of "emotion." The third triad of *Netsah, Hod,* and *Yesod* are the *Sefirot* of "action." *Malkhut*/Shekhinah, represented by the rose, is the world we live in and stands outside the other nine. *Malkhut* has no light of her own and is only able to reflect the energy of the other nine *Sefirot.*

The connection of each of the ten *Sefirot* to one letter of God's name, the Tetragrammaton, is illustrated in this diagram in outlined letters:

keter—point or crown on top of the yod
hokhmah—yod
binah—the first hey
hesed + din + tiferet + netsah + hod + yesod—*vav* (six)
malkhut—the second hey

The verse from 1 Chronicles 29:11-12, which contains references to all of the seven lower *Sefirot,* is found along the bottom semicircle: "Yours, Lord, are greatness (*Hesed/Gedulah*), the might (*Din/Gevurah*), the splendor (*Tiferet*), triumph (*Netzah*), and the majesty (*Hod*), yes, all that is in heaven and on earth (*Yesod*): To

159

You, Lord, belong kingship (*malkhut*/Shekhinah) and preeminence above all."

Keter-Crown

The connotations of *keter*, the first *sefirah*, are found around the circle: *Ehiyeh asher ehiyeh* (the name of God associated with *Keter*); the head, the quality, good; *Adam Kadmon* (the universe of the primeval man); and *yehida* (unique essence, a level of the soul). Emanating from this top circle are found the words from Proverbs 3:19, describing the second two *Sefirot*: "The Lord founded the earth with wisdom and established the heavens with understanding." The fact that even this highest sefirah, however, is not identical to God, who is called *Ein Sof* in Kabbalah (literally, "without limit") is illustrated by the circle of *keter* being cut off at the top, unable to reach God. The color of *keter* is a blinding, invisible white.

Hokhmah-Wisdom

The connotations of *Hokhmah*, the second *sefirah*, are found in its circle: the Tetragrammaton (vocalized as *Elohim*); the brain; the beginning; *atzilut* (the universe of Nearness); and *hiyah* (living essence, a level of the soul). *Hokhmah* is depicted as the upper father, mate of *Binah*, and father of *Tiferet*. *Hokhmah* is connected to all the colors.

Binah-Understanding

The connotations of *Binah*, the third *sefirah*, are found in its circle: *yah* (one of the names of God); the heart; the end; *beriyah* (the world of Creation); and *neshamah* (breath—a level of the soul). *Binah* is depicted as the upper mother, mate of *Ḥokhmah*, and mother of *Tiferet* and all the other *sefirot*. The color associated with Binah is yellow or green.

Ḥesed—Lovingkindness or *Gedulah*—Greatness

Ḥesed, also called *Gedulah*, the fourth *sefirah*, is represented by the biblical personality of Abraham. The tent and the terebinth trees in the center illustrate the verse, found at the bottom of the circle, from Genesis 18:1: "The Lord appeared to him by the terebinths of Mamre; he was sitting at the entrance of the tent as the day grew hot." God's promise to Abraham that he would beget a great nation is portrayed by the twelve stars (twelve tribes) and the verse from Genesis 15:5 at the top of the circle: "Look toward heaven and count the stars, if you are able to count them." Abraham's response to the test of the *Akedah* is found inside the tent—from Genesis 22:1-2: "God put Abraham to the test. He said to him, "Abraham," and he answered, "Here I am." The part of the four species represented by *Ḥesed* is the myrtle, found at the opening of the tent. *Ḥesed's* connection to the element of water is portrayed by the waves at the bottom of the circle and around the outside of the square. *Ḥesed* stands for the first day of creation, shown by the sparks radiating out from the circle, in which are found the words from Genesis 1:3 "Let there be light." Other connotations of *Ḥesed* are included around the circle: El (the name of God associated with *Ḥesed*; the direction, south; the right arm; *ruaḥ* (spirit—a level of the soul); and *Yetzirah* (the universe of formation). The diagram of all ten *Sefirot* in the traditional array is found in the four corners of the picture, with *Ḥesed* highlighted by the Hebrew letter *ḥet*. The color associated with *Ḥesed* is white or silver.

Din—Justice or *Gevurah*—Strength

Din, also called *Gevurah*, the fifth *sefirah*, is represented by the biblical personality of Isaac. The central event in his life, the *Akedah*, is represented by the ram caught in the bushes. The verse from Genesis 22:2 is found on the mountain that Isaac climbed with his father: "Take your son, your favored one, Isaac, whom you love, and go to the land of Moriah, and offer him there as a burnt offering." The component of the four species represented by *Din* is the myrtle branch, seen on either side of the circle. *Din's* connection to the element of fire is portrayed by the flames inside the circle and around the outside of the square. *Din* stands for the second day of creation, shown as the clouds and waves inside the square. Other connotations of *Din* are included around the circle: Elohim (the name of God associated with *Din*); the direction, north; the left arm; fire; blood; *ruaḥ* (spirit—a level of the soul); and *Yetzirah* (the universe of formation). The diagram of all ten *Sefirot* in the traditional array is found in the four corners of the picture, with *Din* highlighted by the Hebrew letter *dalet*. The color associated with *Din* is red or gold.

Tiferet—Beauty

Tiferet is the sixth *sefirah* and holds a central and rich place in the system, representing both the son of *Ḥokhmah* and *Binah* (the second and third *Sefirot*) as well as the husband of Shekhinah, the tenth *sefirah*. Jacob is the biblical character connected with *Tiferet* and is represented by the image of the ladder that he saw in his dream. Jacob's words in Genesis 28:16 are found around the upper half of the inner circle: "Surely God is in this place, and I did not know."
Jacob's dream of wrestling with the angel is referred to in the bottom of this inner circle, with the verse from Genesis 32:29: "Your name shall no more be called Jacob, but Israel." The component of the four species represented by *Tiferet* is the myrtle, which grows

from the central Tree of Life, another important symbol of this *sefirah*. Other connotations of *Tiferet* are found on the rungs of the ladder: light; written Torah; and the sun. *Tiferet* refers to the element of air and to the heavens, represented by the clouds between the circles.

Tiferet's connection to the third day of creation is shown around the square by the images of land and the seven fruits of ancient Israel: olives, dates, grapes, wheat, barley, pomegranates, and figs. Other connotations of *Tiferet* are included around the outer circle: the Tetragrammaton (the name of God associated with *Tiferet*); the direction, east; the torso; *ruah* (spirit—a level of the soul); and *Yetzirah* (the universe of formation). The diagram of all ten Sefirot in the traditional array is found in the four corners of the picture, with *Tiferet* highlighted by the Hebrew letter *tav*. The color associated with *Tiferet* is yellow or purple.

Netzah—Victory

The seventh *sefirah* is *Netzah* or Victory. Moses is the biblical character connected with *Netzah* and is represented by images inside the circle: the burning bush and the giving of the Law at Sinai. On the summit of the mountain are found the words from Exodus 33:11: "And God spoke to Moses face to face" and from Exodus 3:2: "And behold the bush burned with fire, and the bush was not consumed." Willow branches, the part of the four species of Sukkot associated with *Netzah*, grow from the bush. *Netzah* is related to the fourth day of creation, shown here by the sun, moon, and stars surrounding the circle. Other connotations of *Netzah* are written around the circle: *Adonai tzeva'ot* (one of God's names); the direction, up; the left leg; the fourth day; *ruah* (spirit—a level of the soul); and *yetzirah* (the universe of formation). The diagram of all ten *Sefirot* in the traditional array is found in the four corners of the picture, with *Netzah* highlighted by the Hebrew letter *nun*. *Netzah* is represented by the color light pink.

Hod—Splendor

The eighth *sefirah* is *Hod* or Splendor. Aaron is the biblical character connected with *Hod* and is represented by images inside the circle: the menorah from the tabernacle; the hands in the position of blessing; and the words of the priestly blessing found in Numbers 6:24-26: "May the Lord bless you and keep you. May the Lord face you and shine upon you. May the Lord turn to you and give you peace." At the base of the menorah are found the words from Numbers 17:23: "And behold, the rod of Aaron blossomed." These almond flowers surround the menorah and turn into willow branches, the part of the four species connected with *Hod*. *Hod* refers to the fifth day of creation, shown here by the fish and birds around the circle. Aaron's role as peacemaker is alluded to in the olive branches carried by the doves at the top of the image. Other connotations of *Hod* are written around the circle: *Elohim Tzevaot* (one of God's names); the direction, down; the left leg; *ruaḥ* (spirit—a level of the soul); and *Yetzirah* (the universe of formation). The diagram of all ten *Sefirot* in the traditional array is found in the four corners of the picture, with *Hod* highlighted by the Hebrew letter *hey*. *Hod* is represented by the color dark pink.

Yesod—Foundation

The ninth *sefirah* is *Yesod* or Foundation. Joseph, the biblical character connected with *Yesod*, is represented by images inside the circle: Joseph's dreams of his brothers as eleven stalks of wheat bowing to his upright stalk; and of eleven stars, the sun, and moon (his brothers, father, and mother). The stars are set in a rainbow, alluding to the many colors in the coat that Jacob gave to Joseph. Jacob's blessing of his favorite son in Genesis 49:26 is found within the rainbow: "The blessings of your father. . . . may they rest upon the head of Joseph." The palm branch of the *lulav* is a symbol of Joseph, who represents male sexuality. *Yesod* refers to the sixth day of creation, which is shown here by the various animals, all depicted in their male images, around the circle. At the bottom, Joseph's brother Benjamin is portrayed by the wolf. The creation of human beings in the image of God is represented by the verses from the Genesis 1: "And God created man in His image" (around the top); "And behold it was very good" (around the bottom); and "Be fruitful and multiply" (at the sides). Other connotations of Yesod are written around the circle: *El Hai* and *Shaddai* (two of God's names); the direction, down; the left leg; *ruah* (spirit—a level of the soul); and *Yetzirah* (the universe of formation). The diagram of all ten *Sefirot* in the traditional array is found in the four corners of the picture, with *Yesod* highlighted by the Hebrew letter *yod*.

Malkhut—Kingdom or *Shekhinah*—Presence

Malkhut is the tenth and last *sefirah*, and is the one that is most accessible to our world. David is the biblical character connected with *Malkhut* and is represented by the image of the lyre in the center, and the verse: "And David danced with all his strength before the Lord" (Samuel 2, 6:14). The feminine aspect of *Malkhut* is contained in the other name for this *sefirah*—Shekhinah or Presence—which is portrayed as a thirteen-petalled rose. This feminine *sefirah* is also represented by the moon, the sea, and the clouds of glory. The Garden of Eden or orchard, found at the bottom of the circle, is a symbol of *Malkhut*/Shekhinah. The *etrog*, one of the four symbols of Sukkot, is found on the trees in the orchard. Rachel as well as David stands for *Malkhut*/Shekhinah and is referred to in the verse from Jeremiah 31:15, around the top of the circle: "A voice is heard in the Ramah— lamentations, and bitter weeping—Rachel weeping for her children; she refuses to be comforted for her children."

Malkhut/Shekhinah represents the seventh day of creation, Shabbat, and is illustrated around the outside of the circle by two candles, two hallahs formed by stalks of wheat, and the grapes and kiddush cup. Other aspects of this *sefirah* are inscribed around the circle: *Adonai* (the name of God connected to *Malkhut*); evil; the mouth (or female genitalia); the oral Torah; queen; bride; daughter; nefesh (the lowest level of the soul); and *asiyah* (the universe of completion). The word *eretz*, "earth," is found in the *kiddush* cup outside the circle, signifying that all of the *Sefirot*, only *Malkhut*/Shekhinah, has no light of her own, reflecting back the light the other nine *Sefirot*. The diagram of all ten *Sefirot* in the traditional array is found in the four corners of the picture, with *Malkhut* highlighted by the Hebrew letter *mem*. The color associated with *Malkhut*/Shekhinah is dark blue.*

*Much of this information about the Sefirot derives from Aryeh Kaplan: *Inner Space.* Moznaim Publishing Corporation, Jerusalem, 1990.

Glossary

aggadah   The body of classical rabbinical lore, consisting of tales, legends, proverbs, historical traditions, and theological statements; all the material included in the talmudic-midrashic literature that is not legal (halakhic) in nature.

Angel of Death (*malakh hamavet*)   An angel, regarded as an agent of God, but who might pursue his own interest in afflicting humans with death. Developing out of earlier roots, the concept of the Angel of Death emerged in the post-biblical period. A famous talmudic statement (Baba Batra 16a) often quoted in the Zohar, identifies the Angel of Death with Satan and also with the evil inclination in man.

Aramaic   A language, related to Hebrew, that existed in various dialects in the ancient Near East. Both the Babylonian and Jerusalem Talmuds were transmitted in Aramaic; the Zohar was also written in Aramaic, though of an artificial medieval character.

archetypal   Marked by elements, motifs, or patterns that recur in the traditions and literature of a culture or of a number of cultures.

atzilut   The highest of four worlds in the kabbalistic world-picture, the realm of the *Sefirot*.

avodah   Divine service. The term specifically refers to the sacrificial cult and ritual associated with the Tabernacle and with the Temple, but in a broader sense the term refers also to all worship and prayer.

Ein sof   "Without end." The purely infinite, indefinable and indescribable, beyond human grasp, definition, or knowledge. The Divine Being prior to, and transcending, the emanation of the *Sefirot*.

Elijah   (*Eliyahu*) A biblical prophet of the ninth century B.C.E., hence prior to the emergence of the literary prophets. According to II Kings 2:1-11, Elijah did not die, but instead mounted a fiery chariot to heaven. Elijah became the subject of countless folk tales depicting him as one who continues to walk the earth, often as a clandestine figure, assisting the distressed, testing people, and disclosing divine secrets.

emanation   The process whereby the purely infinite state of the Divine Being (*Ein sof*) evolved to bring into being the various *Sefirot*.

encyclopedic Suggesting a totality; encompassing all of history, or the history of the cosmos, from its very beginning through its ultimate redemptive state.

Enuma elish An ancient Babylonian creation epic that was read during the Akitu, the spring festival marking the beginning of the year. It explains the creation of the world as proceeding from a conflict between the Babylonian high god, Marduk, and Tiamat, who represents the sea and the forces of chaos.

eschatological Beliefs relating to the end of days, often associated with crisis and cataclysm believed to mark the end of history and the emergence of a messianic order.

Exile of the Shekhinah The separation of the Shekhinah from the other *Sefirot*, specifically from *tiferet*, that *sefirah* which most distinctly represents a masculine character within the higher realm, and the Shekhinah's captivity at the hands of the demonic forces, the *Sitra aḥra*.

Gehenna Hell. A place of punishment for the wicked following death. The name is derived from *Ge hinnom* (the valley of Hinnom) in the vicinity of Jerusalem, a site identified in the Bible (Jeremiah 7:31) as the scene of child sacrifice.

Hadith Islamic traditions, not found in the Koran, largely relating to the deeds and teachings of Mohammed.

ḥaver, ḥaverim Members of a circle or fellowship consisting of students of mystic teaching.

Heavenly Academy A court or academy in which sages, after death, resume their activity of interpreting the Written and Oral Torah. According to talmudic sources, God is said to participate together with the sages in its debates and proceedings. The Zohar depicts the heavenly academy in its own image as a place where divine mysteries are taught, with the angel Metatron presiding.

Idra rabba "The Large Holy Assembly," a gathering of ten *ḥaverim*, the setting in which Rabbi Simeon bar Yohai, approaching the end of his life, revealed highly esoteric teachings (3:127b-145a).

Idra zuta "The Small Holy Assembly," the smaller assemblage of seven *ḥaverim* who survived the death of three additional colleagues from the Large Holy Assembly. To this smaller gathering, Rabbi Simeon bar Yohai disclosed the most highly esoteric mysteries (3:287b-296b) immediately prior to his death.

Ineffable Name   The Tetragrammaton, a four-consonant name for God. In Kabbalah, mystic significance is attributed to each of its four letters, and the true connection of the letters of the Ineffable Name signifies the unity of the different aspects of the divine.

Kabbalah   The major traditions of Jewish mysticism, those esoteric teachings that emerged in or about the twelfth century, including the theosophical mystic teaching that first appeared, it is thought, in Provence and was later given expression in the Zohar.

kelipot   "Shells." Divine light that fell to the depths and hence assumed a demonic character.

Leviathan   A legendary sea monster. The Leviathan recalls a personification of the forces of chaos opposing or preventing creation in ancient Near Eastern myth. In rabbinical lore, Leviathan will be caught and served at a feast for the righteous as part of an eschatological fulfillment.

Metatron   "Angel of the (divine) countenance" who, in some traditions, serves in a celestial Tabernacle. In the Zohar, Metatron is said to preside over the Heavenly Academy.

Midrash   A creative interpretation of biblical texts. Often midrash tends to focus upon each verse or even each word, scrutinizing it independently of its context in the biblical text. The term refers also to a body of rabbinic literature containing midrashic exegesis.

Midrash hane'elam   An earlier layer of zoharic texts that preceded the larger text of the Zohar.

Pirke derabbi eli'ezer   An aggadic work, generally thought to have been composed in the eighth century, a retelling of the biblical narrative drawing upon rabbinic aggadah but also including narrative elements and comments not found in other sources. The Zohar drew upon the aggadic traditions included in this work in particular.

Primordial Light   The light (based upon Genesis 1:3-5) that preceded the creation of the heavenly bodies and, according to rabbinical aggadah, was then withdrawn to be returned to the righteous at a future time.

pseudepigraphy   The practice of ascribing a writing to a well-known personality of an earlier period.

Ra'aya mehemna   An early imitation of the Zohar included within the text of the Zohar itself.

Raziel   "Secrets of God." An angel.

resurrection The physical revival of the dead. Body and soul rejoined in a revival and renewal of the whole person. A concept championed by the Pharisees, the Resurrection of the Dead (*tehiyat hametim*) became a basic concept in rabbinic thought.

Samael A name for Satan used from later talmudic times; in the Zohar, a personification of the *Sitra ahra*.

Sefer habahir The first known kabbalistic text; appeared in Provence during the latter part of the twelfth century.

Sefirot Aspects of the Divine Being and Personality emanating from its completely infinite and indefinable state.

The Ten Sefirot

Keter "Crown," also "Will," and *ayin* (nothingness).

Binah "Understanding." Mother of the lower *Sefirot*. The divine womb; atonement; the World-to-Come.

Hokhmah "Wisdom." The Primordial Torah.

Din "Judgment." Contains the roots of punishment and of evil (*Sitra ahra*). Also called *Gevurah* (Might).

Hesed "Lovingkindness," "compassion." Also called *Gedulah* (Greatness).

Tiferet "Glory," "compassion." Maintains an equilibrium between Lovingkindness and Judgment. The Written Torah. Male aspect within the higher realm, and mate of the Shekhinah. Father of souls.

Hod "Majesty." Contains roots of prophecy.

Netzah "Forever." Similarly contains roots of prophecy.

Yesod "Foundation". The hidden Primordial Light. Instrumental in divine union between *Tiferet* and *Malkhut*. Also symbolic of the *tsadik*, "Righteous One," who is instrumental in effecting divine union. Symbolized by the male sexual organ.

The Ten Sefirot (continued)

Malkhut/The Shekhinah   Lowest, and predominantly feminine *sefirah*; identified with the Oral Torah, the Community of Israel, and the Seventh Day. Mother of souls, who intercedes on behalf of her children. With the Shekhinah, the silence of the highest dimensions of divinity is broken and gives way to divine speech, and hence is associated with the letters of the alphabet. All the higher *Sefirot* flow into *Malkhut*.

shaman   In many traditional tribal religions, the religious figure believed to be able, through an intense degree of ecstasy, to enter into the higher worlds and then to return to this world.

Shekhinah   The "Divine Presence," a distinctly feminine aspect of the Godhead. See the Ten *Sefirot, Malkhut*.

shevah   "Praise." A genre of legend having as its subject a holy man.

Sitra ahra   "The Other Side." A term signifying the forces of evil, the antithesis of the holy and the divine. The demonic reality, in the zoharic world-picture, becomes more powerful through human sin.

soul   According to the Zohar, the soul is a composite consisting of several different layers: *nefesh, ru'ah, neshamah,* and *nishmat haneshamah*; these range from aspects of the personality closely related to the body and to the imprint of the physical body to the mysterious and sublime substratum of the soul quite beyond human comprehension.

Talmud   The oral tradition or law identified with the law code of the Mishnah, and with the Gemara, a collection of discussions interpreting the Mishnah. The Babylonian and Jerusalem Talmuds, including Gemara from those two centers of ancient Judaism, comprise basic documents of historical Judaism.

theosophy   Secrets of the hidden divine life.

Tikkune Zohar   An imitation of the Zohar that became, in effect, a later stage within zoharic literature.

tsadik   "Righteous." In the Jewish mystic tradition, the word connotes a highly devout and holy person. In Kabbalah it refers also to the ninth sefirah, *Yesod*.

yanuka   A wonder child possessing remarkable erudition and sometimes also having cognitive powers beyond the norm.

Bibliography

Aarne, Antti Amatus. *Types of the Folktale: A Classification and Bibliography.* Helsinki: Academia Scientiarum Fennica, 1961.

Ackerman, James. "Satire and Symbolism in the Song of Jonah." In *Traditions in Transformation: Turning Points in Biblical Faith,* ed. B. Halpern and J. Levenson, 213-46. Winona Lake, Ind.: Eisenbrauns, 1981.

Anatoli, Jacob. *Malmad hatalmidim.* Lyck, 1866.

Astell, Ann W. *The Song of Songs in the Middle Ages.* Ithaca: Cornell University Press, 1990.

Azulai, Abraham. *Or haḥamah* I-IV. Przemysl, 1896-1898.

Baer, Yitzhak. *A History of the Jews in Christian Spain,* 2 vols. Philadelphia: Jewish Publication Society, 1972.

Bahya Ibn Asher. *Kad hakemaḥ.* Lemberg: Kelilat Yofi, 1892.

Band, Arnold J. *Nahman of Bratslav: The Tales.* New York: Ramsey, Toronto: Paulist Press, 1978.

Ben-Yehezkel, Mordecai. *Sefer hama'asiyot,* 6 vols. Tel Aviv: D'vir, 1965.

Ber, Moshe. "Lemekorotav shel hamispar lamed-vav tsadikim," In *Sefer Bar-Ilan* I (Churgin Memorial Volume), 172-176. Ramat-Gan, 1963.

Bereshit rabbati. Ed. Hanokh Albeck. Jerusalem: Mekitse Nirdamim, 1940.

Berger, Jacob, and Israel Berger. *Ateret ya'akov veyisra'el.* Lvov, 1881.

Bickerman, Elias. *Four Strange Books of the Bible: Jonah, Daniel, Koheleth, Esther.* New York: Schocken, 1967.

Bodkin, Maud. *Archetypal Patterns in Poetry: Psychological Studies of Imagination.* Oxford: Oxford University Press, 1934.

Bowers, Robert Hood. *The Legend of Jonah.* The Hague: Martinus Nijhoff, 1971.

Callcott, Frank. *The Supernatural in Early Spanish Literature: Studies in the Works of the Court of Alphonso X, El Sabio.* New York: Instituto de las Españas en los Estados Unidas, 1923.

Campbell, Joseph. *The Hero with a Thousand Faces.* Princeton: Princeton University Press, 1949.

Cassutto, Umberto. *Me' adam ve'ad no'aḥ.* Jerusalem: Magnus Press, 1953.

Cholevius, Carl Leo. *Geschichte der deutschen Poesie nach ihren antiken Elementen.* Leipzig: Brodhaus, 1854.

Cirlot, Juan Eduardo. *A Dictionary of Symbols.* London: Routledge and Kegan Paul, 1962.

Cohen-Aloro, D. *Sod hamalbush umar'e hamal'akh besefer hazohar.* Monologues in Jewish Studies, 13. Jerusalem: Hebrew University, 1987.

————."The Zohar's View of Magic as a Consequence of the Original Sin" (Hebrew). *Da'at* 19 (Summer 1977), 31-65.

Corbin, Henri. *Histoire de la Philosophie Islamique*. Paris: Gallimard, 1964.

Cordovero, Moses. *Or hayakar* (commentary on the Zohar), vol. 1— Jerusalem: Ahuzat-Yisra'el, 1962.

Dan, Joseph. *Hasippur haivri bimei habeinayim*. Jerusalem: Keter, 1974.

————."Min hasemel el hamesumal: lehavanat 'asarah ma'amarim bilti-histori'im al hakabbalah' legershom scholem." *Mehkere yerushalayim bemahshevet yisra'el* 5 (1986): 363ff.

Donne, John. *The Complete Poetry of John Donne*. Ed. John T. Shawcross. London: The Stuart Editions, 1968.

————.*The Poems of John Donne*. Ed. Herbert J. C. Grierson. Oxford: Oxford University Press, 1912.

Eliade, Mircea. *History of Religions*, 2 vols. Chicago: University of Chicago Press, 1971.

————.*Myths, Dreams and Mysteries*. New York: Harper and Row, 1967.

————.*Myths, Rites, Symbols: A Mircea Eliade Reader*. Ed. Wendell C. Beane and William G. Doty, 2 vols. New York: Harper and Row, 1976.

Elstein, Yoav. "The Gregorius Legend: Its Christian Versions and Its Metamorphosis in the Hasidic Tale." *Fabula* 27, nos. 3-4 (1986), 195-215.

Farcasiu, Simina M. "The Exegesis and Iconography of Vision in Gonzola de Berceo's *Vida de Santa Oria*." *Speculum* 61/2 (1986): 305-29.

Ferdowsi (Abu ol-Qasem mansur). *Shah-nameh*. In *The Epic of the Kings*, trans. R. Levy, 221-30. Chicago: University of Chicago Press, 1967.

Frazer, James George. *The Golden Bough: A Study in Magic and Religion*, 12 vols. London: Macmillan, 1907-15.

Friedlander, Gerald, tr. and ed. *Pirke de Rabbi Eliezer*. New York: Hermon Press, 1971.

Frye, Northrop. *Anatomy of Criticism*. Princeton: Princeton University Press, 1957.

Funk, Solomon. *Monumenta Talmudica*, 2 vols. Vienna and Leipzig: Orion-Verlag, 1913.

Galante, Abraham. *Zohare hamah* (commentary on the Zohar). Venice, 1650.

Gasta Romanuran, ubersetzt von Johann Georg Theodor Grasse. Leipzig, 1842.

Gibb, H. A. R. and Kramers, J. H. *Shorter Encyclopedia of Islam: Edited on Behalf of the Royal Netherlands Academy*. Ithaca: Cornell University Press, 1953.

Ginzberg, Louis. *Legends of the Jews*, 7 vols. Philadelphia: Jewish Publication Society, 1954.

Goblet, Eugene d'Alviella. *The Migration of Symbols*. New York: University Books, 1956.

Goldberg, Harriet. "The Literary Portrait of the Child in Castilian Medieval Literature." *Kentucky Review Quarterly* 27 (1980): 11-27.

Goodenough, Erwin R. *Jewish Symbols in the Greco-Roman Period.* 13 vols. Princeton: Princeton University Press, 1953-1968 .

Gotleib, Efraim. *haKabbalah bekitve rabbi baḥya ben asher Ibn Ḥalewa.* Jerusalem: Kiryat Sefer, 1970.

Graetz, Heinrich. *History of the Jews.* 7 vols. Philadelphia: Jewish Publication Society, 1895.

Green, H. Benedict. *The Gospel According to Mathew in the Revised Standard Version: Introduction and Commentary.* The New Clarendon Bible. Oxford: Oxford University Press, 1975.

Halperin, David. *The Faces of the Chariot: Early Jewish Responses to Ezekiel's Vision.* Texte und Studien zum Antiken Judentum 16. Tubingen: J. C. B. Mohr, 1988.

Heller, Sondra Rosyla. *The Characterization of the Virgin Mary in Four Thirteenth-Century Narrative Collections of Miracles.* Ph.D. Dissertation, New York University, 1975.

Heschel, Abraham Joshua. *The Circle of the Baal Shem Tov: Studies in Hasidism.* Ed. Samuel H. Dresner. Chicago: University of Chicago Press, 1985.

Idel, Moshe. *Kabbalah: New Perspectives.* New Haven: Yale University Press, 1988.

———."Reification of Language in Jewish Mysticism." *Mysticism and Language.* Ed. Steven T. Katz. New York and Oxford: Oxford University Press, 1992, 42-79.

Jacob, Benno. *The First Book of the Bible—Genesis.* Ed. and trans. Walter Jacob. New York: Ktav, 1974.

Jellenik, Adolf. *Bet hamidrash.* 6 vols. Jerusalem, 1938.

Jeremias, Alfred. *Babylonisches im Neue Testament.* Leipzig: J. C. Hinrichs, 1905.

———.*Handbuch der altorientalischen Geisteskultur.* Berlin: Walter de Gruyter, 1929.

Jolles, Jacob Zevi ben Naftali. *Kehilat Ya'akov.* Jerusalem: M. A. Zibelman, 1971.

Jones, Joseph. "From Abraham to Andrenio: Observations of the Evolution of the Abraham Legend, Its Diffusion in Spain and Its Relation to the Theme of the Self-Taught Philosopher." *Comparative Literature Studies* 6 (1969): 69-101.

Jung, Carl, and K. Kerenyi. *Essays on a Science of Mythology.* Princeton: Princeton University Press, 1949.

Kasher, Menahem. *Torah shelemah.* Jerusalem and Monsey, N.Y.: The American Biblical Encyclopedia Society, 1938-.

Keller, John Esten. *Gonzalo de Berceo.* New York: Twayne, 1972.

———.*Pious Brief Narrative in Medieval Castilian and Galician Verse, from Berceo to Alphonso X.* Lexington: University Press of Kentucky, 1978.

Klapholz, Israel. *Lamed-vav tzadikim nistarim*, 2 vols. Tel Aviv: Pe'er hasefer, 1968.

Komlós, Ottó. "Jona Legends." In *Études orientales á la mémoire de Paul Hirschler*. Ed. Ottó Komlós, 41-61. Budapest, 1950.

Labi, Simeon. *Ketem paz* (commentary on the Zohar), 2 vols. Leghorn, 1795.

Landes, George M. "The Kerygma of the Book of Jonah." *Interpretation* 21 (1967): pp. 10-31.

————."The 'Three Days and Three Nights' Motif in Jonah 2:1." *Journal of Biblical Literature* 86 (1967): 446-50.

Leibes, Yehuda. "Hamashiah shel hazohar." In *Hare'ayon hameshihi beyisra'el*, 87-234. Jerusalem: Israel National Academy of Sciences, 1982.

————."Ketsad nithaber sefer hazohar." In *Sefer hazohar vedoro*, 1-71.

————."Hashpa'ot notsriyyot al sefer hazohar." *Mehkere yerushalayim bemahshevet yisra'el* 2 (1983):, 43-74.

————.*Perakim bemillon sefer hazohar*. Ph.D. dissertation, Hebrew University, 1977.

————."Yonah ben amitai kemashiah ben yosef." *Mehkere yerushalayim bemahshevet yisra'el* 3 (1983-84): 269-311.

Mach, Rudolf. *Der Zaddik in Talmud und Midrasch*. Leiden: E. J. Brill, 1957.

Margaliot, Reuben, ed. *Sefer habahir*. Jerusalem, 1951.

Matt, Daniel C. *Zohar: The Book of Enlightenment*. New York: Paulist Press, 1983.

Megged, Matti. *Ha'or hanehshakh: arakhim estetiyim besefer hazohar*. Tel Aviv: Sifriat po'alim, 1980.

Migne, J. P. Ed. *Origenis. Patrologia Cursus Completus. Series Graeca. Saeculum* 3. Volume 8. Paris: Seu Petit-Montrouge, 1856.

Moses De Leon. *The Book of the Pomegranate*. Edited and translated by Elliot R. Wolfson. Atlanta: Scholars Press, 1988.

Nahman of Bratzlav. *Sippure hama'asiyot*. Numerous Bratzlav editions beginning with the 1815 edition.

Nasr, Seyyed Hossein. *Three Muslim Sages*. Cambridge, Mass.: Harvard University Press, 1964.

Nepaulsingh, Colbert I. *Toward a History of Literary Composition in Medieval Spain*. Toronto: University of Toronto Press, 1986.

Nigal, Gedaliah. "Concerning a Hasidic Manuscript from the Beginning of the Century" (Hebrew). *Kiryat sefer* 52 (1978): 834-44.

————*Hasiporet hahasidit, toldoteha venoseha*. Jerusalem: Y. Marcus, 1981.

Origen. *Contra Celsum*, tr. and ed. Henry Chadwick. Cambridge: Cambridge University Press, 1965.

Orlinsky, Harry M. *Notes on the New Translation of the Torah*. Philadelphia: Jewish Publication Society, 1969.

Oron, Michele. "Me'omanut haderush shel ba'al hazohar," in *Sefer hazohar vedoro*, 299-310.

———."Kol haneshamah tehalel yah, bitui allegori letfisat hamavet besefer hazohar." In *Dappim leheker hasifrut* (1988): 35-38.

———.*haPeli'ah vehakaneh: yesodot hakabbalah shebahem, emdatam hadatit hevratit vederekh itsuvam hasifrutit.* Ph.D. Dissertation, Hebrew University, 1981.

———."Sippur ha'otiot umekorotav, iyun bemidrash hazohar al otiot ha'alef bet." *Mehkere yerushalayim bemahshevet yisra'el* 3 (1983-84): 97-109.

Pechter, Mordecai. "Ben layla levoker." In *Sefer hazohar vedoro*, 311-346.

Perry, T. Anthony. *Art and Meaning in Berceo's Vida De Santa Oria.* Yale Romanic Series 19 (Second Series). New Haven: Yale University Press, 1968.

Pope, Marvin H. *Song of Songs: A New Translation with Introduction and Commentary (Anchor Bible).* Garden City, N. Y.: Doubleday, 1977.

Pritchard, James B. *Ancient Near Eastern Texts.* Princeton: Princeton University Press, 1955.

Rank, Otto. *The Incest Theme in Literature and Legend.* Trans. Gregory C. Richter. Baltimore: Johns Hopkins University Press, 1992.

Safrin, Jacob Moses. *Damasek eli'ezer* (commentary on the Zohar). 7 vols. Przemlysl: Zufnik, 1902-28.

Scheftelowitz, Isador. "Der Fisch-Symbol in Judentum und Christentum." *Archiv für Religionwissenschaft* 14. Leipzig, 1911.

Schirmann, Hayyim. *haShirah ha'ivrit besefarad uveprovans.* 2 vols. Jerusalem: Mosad Bialik, 1956.

Schmidt, Hans. *Jona: Eine Untersuchung zur vergleichenden Religiongeschichte.* Gottingen: Vandenhoeckh and Ruprecht, 1907.

Scholem, Gershom. *Das Buch Bahir.* Leipzig, 1923.

———.*Major Trends in Jewish Mysticism.* New York: Schocken, 1946.

———.*On the Kabbalah and Its Symbolism.* Trans. Ralph Manheim. New York: Schocken, 1965.

———.*Origins of the Kabbalah.* Ed. R. J. Z.Werblowsky, trans. A. Arkush. Philadelphia and Princeton: The Jewish Publication Society/Princeton University Press, 1987.

———.*Sefer hazohar shel gershom scholem.* Jerusalem: Magnes Press, 1993. *Note:* The publication of Scholem's personal annotations on the Zohar appeared too late to allow substantial use of them in this study.

———."The Tradition of the Thirty-Six Hidden Just Men." *The Messianic Idea in Judaism and Other Essays on Jewish Spirituality*, 251-56. New York: Schocken, 1971.

———.*Two Treatises by Rabbi Moses de Leon* (Hebrew). *Kovets 'al yad* VIII. Jerusalem: Mekitse nirdamim, 1976.

Schreiner, Stefan. "Muhammads Rezeption der Biblischen Jona-Erzahlung." *Judaica* 34 (1978): 149-72.

Seder eliyahu rabbah and Seder elihahu zuta (Tanna d'be Eliahu). Ed. Meir Friedmann. Jerusalem: Bamberger and Wahrman, 1960.

Sefer hapeli'ah. Printed, 1784; Przemysl, 1883.

Sefer hazohar. Ed. R. Margoliuth, 3 vols. Jerusalem, 1964.

Sefer hazohar vedoro. Ed. Joseph Dan. *Mehkere yerushalayim bemahshevet yisra'el* 8. Jerusalem, 1989.

Sefer razi'el. Amsterdam, 1701.

Simpson, William. *The Jonah Legend: A Suggestion of Interpretation*. London: G. Richards, 1899.

Speiser, E. A. "Census and Ritual Expiation in Mari and Israel." *Bulletin of the American Schools of Oriental Research* 149 (1958): 24.

At the Dawn of Civilization: The World History of the Jewish People, ed. E. A. Speiser. New Brunswick: Rutgers University Press, 1964.

Spiegel, Shalom. *The Last Trial: On the Legends and Lore of the Command to Abraham to Offer Isaac as a Sacrifice—The Akedah*. New York: Schocken, 1967.

Stendahl, Krister. *The School of St. Matthew and Its Use of the Old Testament*. Philadelphia: Fortress Press, 1968.

Sugarman, Miriam deCosta. *The Debate between the Body and Soul in Spanish Medieval Literature* (Spanish). Ph.D. Dissertation, Johns Hopkins University, 1967.

Svivelman, Abraham Isaac. *Sippure tsadikim hahadash*. Pietrekov, 1910.

Talmage, Frank. "Apples of Gold: The Inner Meaning of Sacred Texts in Medieval Judaism." In *Jewish Spirituality*, ed. A. Green, 1:313-54. New York: Crossroad Press, 1986.

Thompson, Stith. *Motif Index of Folk Literature*. Helsinki, 1932-1936; Bloomington: Indiana University Press, 1955-58.

Tishby, Isaiah. *Mishnat hazohar*. Vol. 1 (with Fischel Lachover). 1949; Vol 2, 1961. Trans. David. Goldstein, *The Wisdom of the Zohar*. 3 vols. Oxford: Oxford University Press, published for the Littman Library, 1989.

Vickery, John B. *The Literary Impact of the Golden Bough*. Princeton: Princeton University Press, 1973.

Von Rad. D. *Genesis*. Philadelphia, 1972.

Widengren, Geo. *The Ascension of the Apostle and the Heavenly Book*. Uppsala: A. B. Lundequistska Bokhandeln, 1950.

Wilkins, Eitone. *The Rose-garden Game: The Symbolic Background to the European Prayerbeads*. London: Victor Gollancz, 1969.

Wineman, Aryeh. *Beyond Appearances: Stories from the Kabbalistic Ethical Writings*. Philadelphia: Jewish Publication Society, 1988.

———."A Child's Tears and his Father's Resurrection: Narrative Art in the Zohar" (Hebrew). *Proceedings of the Tenth World Congress of Jewish Studies 3:1, Jewish Thought and Literature*, 333-37.

———."The Zohar on Jonah: Radical Retelling or Tradition?" *Hebrew Studies* 31 (1990): 57-69.